Employment Ethics

Redefining the Employer–Employee Relationship

Dr. Travis Schachtner

Published in the United States by FTS Leaders
www.FTSLeaders.com

First paperback edition 2025
Editor: Penny Page
Cover Design: Deborah C. Blanc

Schachtner, Travis
Employment Ethics: Redefining the Employee-Employer Relationship

ISBN 979-8-9928309-1-0
1- Business Ethics. 2- Management. 3- Integrity.

Although this publication is designed to provide accurate information in regard to the subject matter covered, the publisher and the author assume no responsibility for errors, inaccuracies, omissions, or any other inconsistencies herein. This publication is meant as a source of valuable information for the reader. However, it is not meant as a replacement for direct expert assistance. If such a level of assistance is required, the services of a competent professional should be sought.

Table of Contents

Introduction

Most of us have, at some point, had a job that we either didn't care about or actually didn't like. One that we were doing just to get a paycheck. Whether it was a summer job in high school or years spent in construction, manufacturing, trucking, or any other hands-on trade, working for someone else can be seen as a part of life. However, despite how much time we spend on the job, how often do we stop to think about what the relationship between the worker and employer really means?

At its core, employment is a simple transaction: An employer provides financial compensation in exchange for an employee's time, effort, and skills. This transaction is shaped by several factors, such as market conditions, labor laws, industry standards, and most importantly, ethics. Employment ethics are not abstract ideals; they are fundamental principles that establish basic workplace ethics, safety, and sustainability worldwide.

This book explores the often-overlooked aspect of employment ethics, breaking down the transactional relationship between employers and employees to help workers better understand their rights, responsibilities, and the larger systems at play. Regardless of the industry, location, or job type, the principles here apply across the board—from manufacturing plants in the US to construction sites in Australia and service industries in Asia. Understanding these principles is essential for anyone who wants to confidently and clearly establish an ethical work relationship with their employer.

The Employment Relationship: A Transaction, Not a Favor

One of the most persistent misconceptions about work is the idea that employment is a form of benevolence. In other words, an employer is "giving" an employee a job out of goodwill. In reality, employment is a business arrangement where both parties have something valuable to offer. The employer needs labor to produce goods or provide services, and the employee needs financial compensation to support their livelihood. The terms of this exchange are often set differently depending on the perspective being considered.

Employers want to present employment in a way that benefits their bottom line. They emphasize competitive wages, professional growth opportunities, and workplace culture, all while prioritizing cost reduction and profit maximization. Employees, on the other hand, approach employment from a different angle, trying to minimize the time spent working so that they can financially meet all their needs. They can then maximize their time with family and friends or pursue an interest or hobby. These differing priorities, while not initially posing a conflict, can lead to ethical concerns, especially when one side has more power than the other.

For too long, the burden of the employment relationship has been placed exclusively on employees. But what happens when employers do not value their employees' time? Workers are told to be more committed, more adaptable, and more dedicated. At the same time, when employers fail to uphold their ethical obligations, the consequences can be severe. Unsafe working conditions, discrimination, unethical wages, and exploitative policies are not unfortunate realities; they are ethical failures that have real impacts on workers and their families.

Why This Matters to Everyone

Employment ethics are not just an issue for a select group of workers or industries. Whether you are a factory worker, a nurse, a truck driver, a software engineer, or a restaurant server, the principles of employment ethics apply to you. They determine whether your workplace is safe, if you are paid ethically, and if your employer respects your rights. Consider these examples:

- An industrial worker discovers that their child, who lives with them in the surrounding area, has developed cancer due to their employer carelessly dumping carcinogens into the soil, which then seep into the water table and the borehole drinking water.

- A woman is passed over for a promotion due to gender discrimination.

- A construction crew is exposed to hazardous materials without proper protection.

- A supermarket worker is forced to work overtime without ethical compensation.

These are not isolated incidents; they are part of a larger pattern in workplaces worldwide. Understanding employment ethics helps workers recognize something wrong and empowers them to act. This could mean advocating for better conditions, seeking legal recourse, or simply making informed career decisions.

What This Book Offers

This book is designed to provide workers with a clear, accessible guide to employment ethics. It will break down complex ideas into practical concepts using real-world examples to illustrate key points. You do not need a law degree or an economics background to understand these ideas. Employment ethics affect all of us, and knowledge of these issues should be available to everyone.

In the following chapters, you will explore topics such as

- the nature of the employer–employee relationship and how it differs from management and leadership.

- how workplace ethics connect to basic human needs.

- how the workforce's demand for employment ethics leads to regulations and their historical importance.

- how workers can recognize and respond to unethical employment practices.

- the importance of community-supporting wages and how they impact workers and communities.

As you read each chapter, you will better understand how employment ethics shape your work life and what you can do to advocate for ethical treatment in any job. More importantly, you will see that employment ethics are not abstract policies or corporate buzzwords; they are real, tangible factors that affect your daily life, financial stability, and well-being.

It does not matter what your job title is, where you live, or what industry you work in—this book is for you. Understanding employment ethics is not only about knowing your rights, but it is also about ensuring that work is an ethical and equitable exchange, where both employees and employers are held to equitable ethical standards. Are you ready to begin? Let's get started!

Chapter 1:

Current Work Ethic

Marcus is a warehouse worker for a regional distribution center. Every day, he arrives 15 minutes early, helps his coworkers set up for the shift, and finishes each assignment ahead of schedule, even when others are not watching. He is known for his reliability and ability to calmly handle problems when equipment breaks down. His coworkers trust him, his managers rely on him, and his performance sets a quiet but clear standard for others.

Over the years, he experienced a rising cost of living, but his pay raises have been inconsistent and minimal. At first, this was not a big deal. He was making enough to cover all his bills and have some spending money to hang out with friends. He started blaming his bad spending habits on things getting more difficult and tried to buckle down on spending. He stopped going out, moved into a smaller apartment, and worked more overtime, but the backslide was constant. As someone who was raised to believe that his hard work and determination would dictate his success, he was blind to the fact that his employer was exploiting his strong work ethic.

For the longest time, employers only recognized a one-way employment relationship: "I pay and you do what you are told." They expected a high work ethic and loyalty because they pay, and the employee has no right to set any expectations for them. With the rise of unions, employers started to be held to some level of accountability for their unethical employment practices.

Eventually, the demand for accountability became too great for political leaders to ignore, and government agencies were created to hold unethical employers accountable for these practices. However, this has not changed employers' overall perception of employees, and that is what we are redefining in this book—starting with the employers' demands of work ethic and commitment.

The Four Components of Work Ethic

Work ethic is not a vague concept. It can be broken down into tangible, observable behaviors that employers seek and reward. The four foundational components constantly observed and considered are *productivity, reliability, autonomy*, and *collaboration*. These define the expectations of today's workforce and influence how workers are perceived, evaluated, and retained.

Productivity: Efficiency, Output, and Time Management

"An honest day's work for an honest day's pay" is a saying that captures the essence of a fair exchange, where effort and compensation go hand in hand. Productivity is one of the two pillars in the transactional nature of the employment relationship, the other being the wage the employer is paying. For employers, it translates directly to profit, efficiency, and operational flow. Employers need productive workers to complete their tasks with good time management and minimal waste. In essence, anyone and everyone meeting the employer's defined expectations is being productive. Going above and beyond what is defined is a choice for the employed, but usually only benefits the employer's profit margins.

Yet, productivity does not always mean making something. In service and gig work, productivity often looks like balancing quality with urgency. A rideshare driver who safely completes multiple trips during peak hours or a barista who orders and keeps a long line moving while maintaining customer satisfaction are examples of productivity. These moments demand focus, time awareness, and decision-making skills under pressure.

Reliability: Consistency, Punctuality, and Responsibility

Reliability is the quiet cornerstone of every workplace. It shows up in workers' daily decisions: arriving on time, meeting expectations regularly, and being present when needed. For employers, particularly frontline workers in blue-collar, service, trade, or healthcare environments, one unreliable worker can disrupt entire systems:

- a dishwasher calls out repeatedly,

- a restaurant's operations slow down,

- a construction worker misses a shift,

- project timelines stretch, and

- safety risks increase

Employers need reliability in their workforce to maintain workflows and meet client expectations. Reliable employees help build predictability in the workflow, allowing the employer to prepare for the organization's future needs or costs. They can also use this reliability to predict the company's earnings to set and inform shareholders of the projected profits. So, when an employer has a reliable workforce, it can signal to the market that it is an ideal organization for investment.

Autonomy: Problem-Solving, Initiative, and Self-Management

Employers need people who can prepare for the needs of the job, complete tasks without constant direct supervision, and address small problems if they arise. In gig work, autonomy is built into the model: workers decide their hours, navigate customer interactions, and handle logistical issues independently.

Of all the aspects of work ethic, autonomy is the most regulated, overhyped, and least rewarded one—with good reason. For example, a construction worker who starts putting in cabinets in a kitchen could see that they just created more work for the plumber installing the sink drain. Or a maintenance technician who diagnoses and fixes an issue could be undermining an overhaul plan brought forth by management. Or a home health aide who changes the care plan for a patient to make things easier for themselves could be undermining a long-established, successful patient routine.

Employers want employees who practice autonomy within the given boundaries of their position and task. Going beyond that again undermines the productivity of the workflow.

Collaboration: Teamwork, Communication, and Adaptability

By its very nature, employment requires collaboration. Even in an organization with one employee, that employee and the employer are now a team. The larger the organization, the more necessary collaboration becomes. In frontline service industries, especially, collaboration is vital for team and organizational success. In the restaurant industry, the line between smooth service and chaos often depends on how well the front and back staff communicate. In health care and maintenance, the ability to communicate the issue, the symptoms, and potential solutions is vital to address any problem.

The adaptability of each individual is vital for team cohesion. It allows employees to adjust when coworkers are absent, plans change, or systems fail. In blue-collar environments, where unpredictability is common, workers who can collaborate under pressure are essential. Without adaptability, any unforeseen problem will cause the team to collapse, because the members will seek excuses or blame shift instead of finding solutions.

Understanding the components of work ethic gives us a clear picture of what basic ethical expectations an employer has set for the employee. However, knowing how employers use these traits in their decision-making is key. It is essential to understand how employers, intentionally or not, exploit employees' work ethic through the additional demand of loyalty, otherwise known as organizational commitment. Knowing these elements will help you get a clearer picture of how one-sided the demand truly is and see that this, in fact, is where the relationship between employer and employee reveals its ethical tensions.

Exploitation of Commitment

Loyalty is often praised by employers as a critical success component. Job listings regularly include phrases like "family," "team player," "dedicated," and "willingness to go above and beyond." The catch is that a high work ethic combined with high commitment is something that employers can exploit. An employee willing to take on more duties even though the employer does not need to provide proper support, compensation, or ethical treatment only increases the employer's profit margins.

When employers discuss how loyal their workforce is to the organization, they are actually discussing their workforce's organizational commitment. The irony is that while loyalty is about why people stay, organizational commitment looks at the burdens created by leaving. This is a long-studied aspect of human resources, consisting of three primary aspects: need, want, and ought.

Need: Burden of the Golden Handcuffs

When looking at the need to stay, the employee is balancing the financial and time costs associated with getting a new job compared to what they are currently making. This is not just a wages and benefits calculation, but includes assessing the change in the cost of living, actual costs to move, how long one could last if the job goes away or doesn't work out, and also addressing any additional education requirements. It is also about considering all the stresses that come with these considerations. When employees believe they can't pursue better professional opportunities due to the calculated costs associated with them, they can also feel the golden handcuffs locking them in place. When looking at work ethic, employees can be exploited by unethical employers by offering wages that do not reflect their productivity.

Ana, a cashier at a local store, feels she is ready for more responsibility and wants to move into a shift manager role. However, it appears that the store managers are content where they are, and she lives in a rural community, so there is little chance for her to find an opportunity without moving. She is making a decent living where she is because the cost of living is low. Does she stay at her current place of employment because she is loyal or because her options are financially limited?

Ought: Burden of Relationship

Some feel that seeking out employment elsewhere is turning their backs on the friendships that they developed and the investments that the organization has made. Even if it is in their best interest, they feel shame for even considering such a thing. Unethical employers may openly exploit these relationships, sacrificing the reliability and collaboration of employees and eroding these relationships to avoid going through the unknown of the hiring and training process of a new employee.

Desmond knows that the warehouse shift manager is a jerk, but when he stood up to him, he became the hero of the floor. His wife informed him of a new position at another company that would be a promotion and a pay raise. But if he leaves, who is going to stand up to the warehouse manager when they go too far? Who is going to train the new hires on floor operations? So, no, he is going to stay; he doesn't need the money that badly. Is this company loyalty, or is he trying to protect the image that others have of him?

Want: The Burden of Pride

Those who have been with an organization for a long time, or are working for organizations they believe have a good reputation, want to stay there. This is the highest form of organizational commitment and usually takes the most time to develop, but once developed, it is the hardest to fight against. The organization is a point of pride that they identify with. Because of its nature, unethical employers exploit this by abusing their workforce's autonomy. An employer that enforces a "do more with less" mentality depends on those with the most pride in their workforce stepping up to fill in the gaps and shoulder more responsibilities without proper compensation.

Carlos is working for the same window manufacturing company that his father and grandfather worked for. Through the years, he has moved from the floor to team lead, and is now a supervisor of three production lines for the third shift. However, the company was recently bought out, and "cost-saving" measures were implemented. One of the cost-saving measures was the layoffs of line workers, leads, and supervisors. Now, instead of ensuring that his 3 slightly understaffed production lines were running smoothly, he is dealing with 10 drastically understaffed ones. He has consolidated the crews but is not hitting the quotas established before the cuts. He reminds himself regularly of the generational time his family has invested in the company as a reason not to quit. Is he staying in the environment out of loyalty, or is his pride in what was preventing him from moving on?

Reflection: Does Your Workplace Appreciate Work Ethic?

Work ethic is given a lot of lip service, but is not always supported ethically. It's important to take a moment to assess whether your workplace truly values your effort. It simply depends on it without offering ethical treatment in return. Ethical employers create conditions that nurture work ethic through respect, recognition, and reciprocity. Use the following questions to reflect on how your employer views and responds to work ethic in your role:

- *Are your contributions consistently acknowledged or rewarded when you demonstrate exceptional effort or performance?*

- *Do you feel that your time, productivity, and reliability are matched with ethical compensation or support?*

- *When you take initiative or independently solve problems, is this encouraged or taken for granted?*

- *Are your ideas and input respected in team settings, even if you are not in a leadership role?*

- *Do you feel comfortable setting boundaries without fear of being labeled as "lazy" or "uncommitted?"*

- *Is your workload manageable, or does your employer rely too heavily on your willingness to go the extra mile?*

- *Does your company offer training or growth opportunities that help build your autonomy and collaboration skills?*

- *Are expectations around teamwork and communication clear, and are they applied fairly to everyone?*

- *Do your managers or supervisors lead by example when it comes to work ethic, or do they rely on others to pick up the slack?*

- *Would you recommend your workplace to someone else based on how they treat employees?*

Think about the answers you have given; it might be the case that your employer is benefiting from your work ethic without creating an environment that ethically supports it. Recognizing these imbalances is the first step in advocating for change. This can be done through conversations, setting boundaries, or seeking new opportunities where your efforts are truly valued. *But what about those who are responsible for valuing us? Are they leaders or are they managers?* In the next chapter, you will explore the differences between them and why it matters.

Chapter 2:

Employers Are Not

Leaders

When Jake started his new job at a manufacturing plant, he believed his supervisor had his back. On his first day, the supervisor shook his hand and told him he was now "a part of the family." Jake was assured his hard work would lead to promotions and job security, and he took those words to heart. He showed up early, took on extra shifts, and never questioned company policies. When safety protocols were ignored to sustain production demands, he assumed it must be a part of the job. When his paycheck was missing his overtime pay, he trusted that management would fix it eventually.

Months passed, and Jake started to notice a pattern. Overtime issues were never solved, safety concerns were brushed off, and when layoffs came, loyalty meant nothing. He knew his supervisor was a leader and had his back, but the supervisor was eventually replaced by someone who was more of a "team player." It's not that his supervisor didn't have his back, but rather that his employer didn't care. Jake then realized that his supervisor was not a leader, but another representative of the company's interests.

Stories like Jake's are common, and it might have happened to you at some point—perhaps it is going on right now. This is because many workers assume their employer or even their direct manager is a leader in the way a mentor or coach might be. In reality, it is essential to understand that employment is a transactional relationship, not a personal commitment. Employers provide wages in exchange for labor, but that does not mean they are invested in their employees' growth or well-being.

This chapter will start you on understanding employment ethics by breaking down why employment is not the same as leadership, why this distinction matters, and how understanding the true nature of the employer–employee relationship can help workers manage their careers with clarity. Not all managers or employers are leaders, and assuming they are can be a costly mistake.

Defining the Employer–Employee Relationship

It is often the case that people enter the workforce believing that their employer's role is to guide, support, and develop them professionally. While some companies do foster growth and mentorship, the fundamental nature of employment is not based on leadership—it is a transaction. The employer–employee relationship is built on an exchange in which the worker provides labor, skills, and productivity, while the employer provides financial compensation in the form of wages and benefits.

This distinction is essential to understanding employment ethics. Unlike a leadership relationship, which is built on mutual trust, employment is structured around business needs and financial goals.

Work vs. Employer vs. Employment Ethics

It is important to understand the difference between *work ethics, employer ethics,* and *employment ethics.* These terms are often confused or used interchangeably, although they represent distinct aspects of the employment relationship.:

- **Work ethics** are the behaviors and values all employers expect from their workforce and are often used as metrics to evaluate performance. The primary characteristics of employee ethics are productivity, reliability, autonomy, and collaboration.

- **Employer ethics** are the behaviors and values that the entire workforce expects from their employers, and which they are historically required to legally enforce. These include a safe and secure workspace, a professional relationship, environmental responsibility, and a community-supporting wage. Just as workers are expected to uphold their work ethics, employers are expected to do the same with employer ethics.

- **Employment ethics** represents the dynamic relationship between work ethic and employer ethics. When both parties are actively trying to meet the demands of the other, that is an ethical workplace.

These definitions illustrate how employment is a transaction between two parties and not a leader–follower relationship. It becomes easier to see the competing interests of both parties and where ethical challenges can arise between them. With this in mind, let's explore how wages, benefits, and productivity shape this dynamic and why assuming good faith from both sides can sometimes lead to unexpected consequences.

Employment as a Transaction

Employment is not a gift or a favor. It is a contractual exchange. The company pays an employee based on the value of their work, and, in return, the employee commits their time and skills. Currently, this transaction is influenced by factors such as market demand, industry wages, and labor laws.

While this system can function ethically, it also creates room for ethical concerns. Employers aim to maximize efficiency and minimize costs, which can sometimes lead to profit-prioritization practices over workforce health and well-being. Likewise, employees might feel pressured to overextend themselves, accepting unethical conditions due to the necessity to meet their personal and familial needs. Both sides often assume the other will act ethically, but ultimately, there is no guarantee of this.

Why Employment Is Not Leadership

One of the most common misconceptions in the workplace is the belief that managers or employers are natural leaders. However, as will be highlighted later, leaders and managers require different skills and have distinct sources of power. Zaleznik (2004) explains that managers focus on structure, processes, and business efficiency, instinctively working to solve problems quickly. On the other hand, leaders focus on people and are necessary in times of crisis, conflict, controversy, or change.

As you will see in the next section, this distinction matters because leadership involves a deeper level of responsibility to people, while employment operates within a framework of business interests. A boss may offer encouragement, but that does not necessarily mean they have the employee's best interests at heart. Workers who assume ethical leadership from their employer risk misunderstanding the nature of their job security, compensation, and workplace treatment. By recognizing that employment is transactional and not necessarily based on ethical leadership, workers can better manage their careers, advocate for their rights, and make informed decisions about their professional future.

Why This Distinction Matters

It is easy to assume that employers—or even direct managers—will always act in the best interest of their employees. Many workers go into a job expecting their employer to be a guiding force—a leader who values their well-being as much as their productivity. However, this assumption can be misleading and even dangerous.

Reality of Employment vs. Leadership

We've established thus far that a common misconception in the workplace is that employers or managers automatically embody leadership qualities. While some do, employment itself does not guarantee leadership. Employers may emphasize the importance of leadership skills, but when it comes to a promotion, it is the management skills that one has that employers value the most. This is because an employer's primary role is ensuring that the business runs smoothly, not necessarily mentoring or advocating for employees.

This distinction is crucial because workers who mistakenly view their employer as a leader may develop unrealistic expectations. They might assume their company will act in their best interest, prioritize employee well-being, or provide career growth opportunities. When these expectations are unmet, employees may feel disillusioned, undervalued, or even exploited. Understanding this difference can help workers make more informed career choices and deal with workplace dynamics more effectively.

Employer's Motivations: Profit and Market Competitiveness

Employers operate within a framework dictated by market competition, industry standards, and financial objectives. Their main goal is to maximize profits. This focus does not inherently make them unethical, but when the focus of the employer shifts from long-term business stability to short-term financial gains, unethical decision-making becomes more likely.

For employees, it means that their well-being is less valuable than the short-term perception of financial viability. Layoffs, wage freezes, and benefit reduction actions that used to destroy businesses because they were seen as signs highlighting financial weakness are now commonplace because employers' perception of short-term gains has become more important than long-term viability. Overall, managers are responsible for meeting key performance indicators and organizational objectives, sometimes at the expense of employee satisfaction (Greenhalgh, 2023).

This is not to say that all employers disregard ethics, but it highlights why employees must advocate for their own interests. A company may offer competitive wages and benefits not out of goodwill; rather, they are choosing to be passive in how they set their wages, and the labor market allows it. Likewise, ethical labor practices are often a response to legal requirements or public pressure rather than a voluntary commitment to ethics.

Why Employees Should Not Assume Ethical Leadership

When employees assume that their employer is a leader, they may overlook signs of unethical behavior or fail to push for better conditions. This can lead to several negative consequences, such as

- **Unethical treatment going unchallenged:** Employees may hesitate to question company policies, assuming they are in place for their benefit when they primarily serve the employer's interests.

- **Overreliance on employer-provided opportunities:** Workers might wait for career growth opportunities instead of actively seeking better wages and promotions.

- **Blind loyalty:** Employees who believe their employer is a leader may remain at a company despite exploitative practices, assuming things will eventually improve.

Here are five examples that help illustrate these situations:

1. Sarah has worked in a manufacturing plant for five years. She consistently meets her quotas, takes on extra shifts, and trains new employees.

Her manager frequently praises her work ethic, but when she asks for a raise, she is told, "You should be grateful to have a job in this economy." She wonders if her employer values her dedication. Ask yourself, *Is Sarah being recognized ethically for their contributions or is she being taken advantage of?*

2. James works in construction and has been with the company for nearly a decade. One day, he and several coworkers are laid off with little warning. The company is still making profits, but the CEO explains that cutting labor costs will help maintain competitiveness. Ask yourself, *Did the employer make this decision based on ethical leadership or financial goals?*

3. Alex has been a supervisor at a retail store for three years. He has been promised a promotion multiple times but continues to see external hires fill higher positions. When he asks his employer about career advancement, he is simply told, "You need to be patient." Ask yourself, *Is Alex's employer genuinely invested in his growth, or is he being strung along?*

4. Maria works in a warehouse where safety measures are frequently ignored to meet deadlines. One day, she witnesses a coworker get injured due to the lack of proper equipment. When she raises concerns, her manager dismisses them, saying, "That's just how the industry works." Ask yourself, *Is Maria's employer prioritizing profit over worker safety?*

5. Tom's boss frequently refers to the workplace as a "family," encouraging employees to work late without extra pay and to "go the extra mile" for the company. Tom starts feeling guilty for taking days off, even when he is sick. Ask yourself, *Is Tom's employer using emotional manipulation to extract more labor without compensation?*

In all cases, how does the attitude of the employer differ from the attitude a leader would have? By reflecting on these examples, it is possible to start making important distinctions between leaders and managers. This brings us to the reflect: If employers are not necessarily leaders, why do so many workers believe otherwise? How do companies encourage blind loyalty, and why do employees often feel indebted to their jobs? To help you better understand these misconceptions, including the romance of leadership theory, the next section will explore the matter deeper.

Potential Misconceptions

The belief that a company has the employees' best interests at heart is not uncommon. This is often encouraged by corporate messaging, workplace culture, and even societal norms that depict companies as benevolent opportunity providers. At the same time, this perception might not always align with reality. It is essential to remember that a company's primary obligations are to its financial stakeholders and not its workforce.

Understanding the difference between employer, manager, and leader helps us assess our workplace environment and determine if we are dealing with ethical leadership or simply employment management. Here is a table that can be used to help better understand if there are any potential misconceptions about how you perceive the workplace:

Category	Employer	Manager	Leader
Primary focus	business profitability	resource management and the day-to-day operations	address crisis, conflict, controversy, or change
Decision-making	based on financial interests	based on company policies and departmental objectives	based on achieving a known shared vision of the future
Ethical responsibility	compliance with labor laws and regulations	implementing company rules and ensuring smooth workflow	ensure the well-being of their followers and their trust

Relationship with employees	transactional (work exchanged for wages)	supervisory (ensuring tasks are completed)	informal (often unrecognized)
Motivation for fair treatment	Legal requirements and reputation management	meeting performance benchmarks and department goals	genuine concern for their peers' growth and well-being
Employee perspective	"I work for them."	"They direct my work."	"They help me."

Myth of the Benevolent Employer

Many companies present themselves as more than just a workplace. They brand themselves as families, communities, or even benevolent forces in the employees' lives. This messaging, while comforting, can be misleading. The idea of a "benevolent employer" suggests that companies are naturally generous, prioritizing employee well-being over profits. In reality, businesses operate under financial constraints, market pressures, and shareholder expectations that often conflict with employee needs.

According to Saval (2015), businesses are not structured to be charitable entities, and believing that they "act in their workers' best interests is to misunderstand the nature of the firm in the contemporary capitalist economy." Decisions regarding wages, benefits, and career development opportunities are offered not out of kindness but as strategic acts to maintain a competitive edge. Companies invest in their employees when it aligns with their goals, but may withdraw support when profits decline.

A corporation might implement generous parental leave when competing for top talent but later roll back on these benefits during a financial downturn. A company may promote a culture of work–life balance while quietly rewarding employees who work overtime without pay. These contractions reveal that an employer's primary concern is maintaining a productive and cost-effective workforce rather than employing and maintaining strong employer ethics.

Romance of Leadership: Why We Overestimate Employer Integrity

The romance of leadership (ROL) theory, developed by Menidl, Ehrlich, and Dukerich (1985), explains how people tend to overattribute organizational success or failure to individual leaders. This cognitive bias leads employees to perceive strong, charismatic managers or CEOs as the primary driving force behind a company's ethical and operational decisions. In reality, however, leaders often function within broader corporate and economic constraints, making decisions that prioritize profitability over employee well-being.

This overestimation of leadership integrity is reinforced through corporate storytelling. Leaders are often depicted as selfless pioneers who overcome obstacles to protect their employees, drive success, and create meaningful change. Employees, in turn, develop a sense of trust and admiration, believing that working under such leadership guarantees ethical treatment. While inspiring leadership can be a powerful motivator, this idealized perception can also create unrealistic expectations and cause employees to overlook systemic issues within the organization.

ROL can manifest in the workplace in different ways, some of them being:

- **The charismatic CEO as a moral figure:** Many companies market their leaders as ethical visionaries, emphasizing their commitment to progressive values, diversity, and employee well-being. These people focus on cultivating strong public personas that mix business acumen with a sense of mission and should be examples of success attribution. However, despite their visionary status, these individuals have made decisions, such as mass layoffs, union suppression, and cost-cutting measures, that reflect corporate priorities rather than ethical leadership.

- **Success attribution bias:** Employees often credit a company's success to its leadership, assuming that ethical leadership naturally translates to long-term job security and ethical treatment. At the same time, external factors such as market conditions, competition, and investor pressure play significant roles in shaping business outcomes. When businesses struggle, employees may feel shocked or betrayed by leadership decisions that prioritize cost-cutting over workforce stability, even though these decisions align with corporate survival strategies.

- **The "family" illusion:** Many companies reinforce the ROL by branding themselves as tight-knit communities or "work families." This creates an emotional bond between employees and leadership, making it harder for workers to critically assess decisions that negatively impact them. Employees who believe in this narrative may hesitate to advocate for themselves, assuming their employer will naturally look out for their best interests.

Reflection Section: How Do You Perceive Your Current Employment Situation?

As you move forward in this book, it is important to take a step back and assess how you currently view your employment relationship. Many employees assume their workplace functions ethically and that their employers naturally have their best interests at heart. As you have explored in this chapter, employment is a transactional arrangement, and leadership is not always a synonym for ethical responsibility.

The following questions will help you reflect on your perceptions of your employer, leadership, and workplace dynamics. Your answers can serve as a guide for how you engage with the concepts in this book. Be honest with yourself; there are no right or wrong answers, only insights that will help you better perceive your workplace, manage your career, and advocate for yourself in the workplace.

- *Do you believe your employer genuinely cares about your well-being, or do they primarily focus on productivity and profits?*

- *Have you ever hesitated to ask for a raise, promotion, or better working conditions because you assumed your employer would eventually reward you for your loyalty?*

- *If your employer had to choose between maintaining employee benefits and increasing shareholder profits, which do you think they would prioritize?*

- *Have you ever stayed at a job longer than you should have because you felt personally loyal to your employer, even when better opportunities were available?*

- *Do you believe that being a hardworking, ethical employee guarantees job security, or do you recognize that external factors and business priorities often determine employment stability?*

- *When evaluating your job satisfaction, do you focus more on how leadership makes you feel or on tangible benefits like ethical pay, work–life balance, and job security?*

After answering these questions, take a moment to reflect on any patterns in your responses. Are you viewing your workplace through an idealistic lens, or do you recognize the realities of employment? The way you perceive your employer–employee relationship will influence how you read this book. If you find that you are operating under assumptions of leadership benevolence or unconditional job security, consider how this perspective might shape your career decisions moving forward.

At its core, people do not work because they want to; it is all connected to fundamental needs. They do not show up just because of their paycheck; they seek stability, security, and fulfillment. Understanding why workers tolerate unethical conditions or feel loyalty to an employer despite unethical treatment requires a deeper look into human motivation. In the next chapter, you will explore how Maslow's Hierarchy of Needs applies to the modern workforce, examining how employment meets (or fails to meet) employees' psychological and practical needs.

Chapter 3:

Understanding Needs

Imagine walking into work daily knowing your financial stability, personal safety, and sense of belonging are secure. You feel valued, respected, valued, and motivated because your workplace supports your needs just beyond a paycheck. Now, imagine the opposite: walking into an environment filled with uncertainty, where job security is fragile, management is indifferent to your well-being, and ethical concerns are dismissed. The difference between these two experiences is more than workplace culture—it is about whether fundamental human needs are met.

Throughout history, people have relied upon their jobs to fulfill far more than financial obligations. Work provides structure, identity, social interaction, and ideally, a sense of purpose. This link to one's job is so strong that in ancient cultures, it was adopted as part of their name. However, many employees struggle with workplaces that fail to meet even their basic needs. To make this situation even more challenging, employees fear that reporting unethical or improper behavior will lead to retribution or that speaking up will not matter, which prevents them from speaking up (Wetherell & Pendell, 2022). In most cases, the reason for dissatisfaction includes a lack of ethical leadership, job stability, or even personal fulfillment.

Employment ethics and job satisfaction are directly linked. When employees feel secure, valued, treated ethically, and can support their community, they perform better, remain more engaged, and are less likely to experience burnout. At the same time, when ethical concerns are ignored and basic needs are overlooked, productivity suffers and turnover rates increase. Employers who are passive about their ethical duties have a harder time retaining talent and may even suffer legal consequences due to these practices, which we will explore later in this book.

In this chapter, you will see how employment ethics connect to fundamental human needs, using Maslow's Hierarchy of Needs as a framework. By understanding this model of motivation, you will be able to evaluate if your job fulfills essential needs better and identify areas where the employer may be falling short. Ultimately, recognizing these gaps will empower you to make informed decisions about your career and advocate for more ethical workplaces.

Maslow's Hierarchy of Needs

Maslow's Hierarchy of Needs is one of the most well-known psychological theories in human motivation, introduced by Abraham Maslow in 1943. It proposed that individuals have a set of needs arranged in a soft hierarchical structure, meaning that usually the more fundamental needs must be met relatively before higher-level aspirations can be recognized, missed, and then pursued. The key resource needed to meet every need is time. The more time one must spend working to achieve their lower-level needs, the less time one will have to dedicate to achieving higher ones. This framework, while focused on personal motivation and highlighting the importance of freedom of choice, has significant applications for modern employment ethics.

The Five Levels of Maslow's Hierarchy

Maslow's model is often represented as a pyramid, with basic survival needs at the bottom and self-fulfillment at the top. Each level builds on the previous one, forming a structured approach to human motivation. The first two needs, Physiological and Safety & Security, form what is referred to as the basic needs, and the other three form the higher needs. Starting from the bottom up, this is what the structure would look like:

1. **Physiological needs:** These are the most basic human requirements, such as food, water, shelter, and rest. In the context of employment, wages play a direct role in satisfying these needs. Passive employer ethics lead to employees struggling to afford necessities, leading to stress, reduced productivity, and ultimately, high turnover rates. Employers who actively ignore the cost of living of their workforce and fail to provide a predictable income create environments where employees are constantly in survival mode, unable to focus on any personal, familial, and professional growth.

2. **Safety and Security needs:** At this level, people focus on securing their basic needs for the long term and are relatively safe from harm. In modern society, this is a stable income, insurance, and the ability to save for emergencies. Ethical employers recognize that stability fosters employee loyalty and higher engagement, while unethical practices, such as sudden layoffs, exploitative contracts, or unsafe conditions, are seen as threats to one's safety and create constant anxiety. Consider an employee working for a company with a history of arbitrary terminations; this uncertainty can breed a culture of fear, reducing morale and productivity.

3. **Love and Belonging needs:** Humans crave social connections, whether through friendships, family, or workplace relationships. When organizations actively strive to meet the ethical demands of the workforce, it becomes easier for the workforce to fulfill their need of belonging through their employer. Employers who neglect their ethical duties allow a disconnect to be established in the employee–employer relationship. That disconnect will force the employee to look to other avenues to get their need for belonging met.

4. **Esteem needs:** Employers foster this need through promotions, performance evaluations, and opportunities for professional growth. It is through esteem that motivation beyond basic needs is fostered, and organizations can

responsibly take risks with workforce support. When esteem is not encouraged or is seen with resentment, organizational stagnation is the norm because all potential change is seen as a threat to the basic needs. An employee who consistently exceeds expectations, for example, but doesn't receive a higher-than-cost-of-living wage increase, is having their search for esteem undermined and will seek to fulfill it elsewhere.

5. **Self-actualization:** At the peak of the hierarchy, self-actualization is often referred to as being in the zone. Employees within an organization are often seen as problem solvers and leaders within their line of work. There is rarely a formal title, and within an organization, they are just considered the best at a specific task or job by management and their peers. Self-actualization is most often experienced through one's hobbies but is often identified as working at one's personal peak without being shackled by anxiety and fears negatively associated with other needs.

While Maslow's hierarchy is often discussed in psychological contexts, its application to the workplace is a valid and crucial analysis that should be made. Employees perform best when their fundamental needs are met, and failure to address these needs can result in disastrous consequences. Imagine a company that offers high salaries but maintains a toxic work environment, where employees feel unsafe or unsupported. Despite having their physical needs met, these workers may struggle with safety and belonging, leading to high turnover rates.

Society's Role in Meeting Needs

Maslow also acknowledged that societal structures play a role in empowering individuals to meet their needs. Governments, businesses, and institutions all have a responsibility to create environments that promote well-being. Labor laws, workplace safety regulations, and ethical business practices contribute to a society where employees can thrive. Ethical employers who acknowledge this responsibility contribute to employee well-being and a more stable and productive workplace.

When employers fail to adequately support these needs, they create environments where employees are forced to make difficult trade-offs, such as choosing between financial security and mental well-being, or between job stability and ethical concerns. Recognizing when an employer refuses to actively ensure that their employees' basic needs are being responsibly met then those employees will seek alternatives that align with their values and goals.

By understanding Maslow's hierarchy, employees can better assess their workplace experiences, recognizing if their needs are being met and where improvements are necessary. *But how does the Maslow Hierarchy of Needs apply to workplace ethics?* In the next section and throughout the remainder of the book, you will explore how these needs translate directly into the employment relationship and how ethical concerns can arise when they are ignored.

Applying Maslow to Employer Ethics

Using the framework explained before, you can establish a relationship between needs and employer ethics. To understand this concept, it is essential to remember that employment is a transactional exchange of labor for wages, where ethical considerations directly impact an employee's ability to thrive. When employers fail to acknowledge their role in fulfilling these fundamental human needs, workplace ethical concerns arise. By applying the framework to employer ethics, you can identify areas in which companies must be active participants in the workplace ethics relationship.

As you will see, the same structure that you have seen before can be applied to the same pyramid of needs. While you will explore each of these in more detail in the next chapters, this section provides an overview of how Maslow's Hierarchy of Needs would apply to workplace ethics.

Employer Ethics and Well-Being

The old adage you have already seen in Chapter 1, "An honest day's pay for an honest day's work," highlights the two-way nature of employment ethics. Each party is the judge of the other's actions, and when both parties are actively trying to meet the basic ethical expectations of the other, both parties can succeed. While employees are expected to demonstrate a high level of work ethic, employers historically refused to reciprocate with an equally high level of employer ethics. Employers fail to realize that a high employer ethic leads to a high work ethic and a higher well-being for both parties.

An example of this would be an organization that emphasizes work ethic but simultaneously disregards employee well-being, resulting in a culture of burnout rather than productivity. When a company constantly depends on employees working long hours, it hinders work ethic. With a lack of rest, professional development, or work–life balance, employees may feel frustrated, and anxiety builds. Employment ethics recognize that productivity is not just about working harder; it is also about fostering a culture where employees can sustain their efforts over the long term.

Resource Confusion: The Disconnect Between Employee Time and Employer Costs

It is essential to remember that one of the most significant ethical dilemmas in employment is the disparity in how employees and employers perceive their resources. As stated previously, employers prioritize financial efficiency, seeking to maximize productivity while minimizing labor costs. Employees, however, value their personal time, viewing work as an exchange of giving effort for a certain amount of time for ethical compensation

This creates an ethical dilemma because both parties value these resources differently. The employee needs the employer to maintain a level of financial viability to ensure their employment continues, but the employer does not need to value the employee's personal time. When employers stop valuing the employees' time, it undermines the basic agreement of the employer–employee relationship. This creates the natural argument for the erosion of work ethic within an unethical employer's workforce over the long term. Ethical workplaces acknowledge that employee time is just as valuable as company profits and strive to create equitable work structures that respect both resources.

Why This Matters

As an employee, you dedicate a significant portion of your time and energy to the job. The vast majority of people want to take pride in everything that they do, and that includes work. To do so, some basic expectations need to be met. But what happens when these expectations are not met? What if your workplace is quietly failing to support your basic needs? Recognizing ethical gaps in employment is not always straightforward. Many employees endure unethical conditions because they have been conditioned to believe it is "part of the job." However, understanding when your employer's ethics are falling short is the first step in advocating for change and improving your professional well-being. Recognizing these shortcomings and understanding your rights can empower you to advocate for a more ethical workplace.

Workplace ethics extend beyond just following the law. They shape the culture, expectations, and long-term sustainability of a company. When an employer fails to meet basic ethical standards, the consequences ripple through the workforce. The following key areas: workplace safety, accountability in professional relationships, corporate responsibility, and community-supporting wages are essential in determining whether your employer is upholding ethical obligations. Each will be delved into more deeply later in this book.

- **Safe and secure workplace:** Workplace safety is a fundamental right, but not all employers prioritize it. Safety isn't limited to physical protection from hazards; it also includes job security and freedom from a toxic or hostile work environment. Ethical workplaces foster a culture of safety by enforcing policies, offering proper training, and ensuring employees feel secure in their roles.

- **Accountable professional relationship:** Trust in leadership or management is built on accountability and transparency. Ethical workplaces ensure that promotions, discipline, and company policies are consistently and ethically applied. However, some organizations operate with favoritism, vague policies, or inconsistent rule enforcement, leading to employee frustration.

- **Responsible impact on the surrounding environment:** The ethical responsibilities of a company extend beyond its employees. Businesses impact their communities and the environment, and ethical employers understand that a strong, well-educated community living in a well-maintained environment creates a long-lasting organization.

- **Community-supporting wage:** One's wage is not just a financial issue: It is also an ethical obligation. Employers who pay unethical wages contribute to the financial instability of the community they depend on for workers. Ethical employers monitor the cost of living in the regions where they employ and the cost of education they require and adjust their wages accordingly.

Recognizing ethical workplace gaps is the first step toward meaningful change. By assessing your work environment through the lens of these pillars, it is possible to determine if your employer is upholding ethical standards or falling short. At the same time, it is important to remember that advocating for change does not always mean directly confronting leadership. It can start with small actions such as setting boundaries, seeking support from coworkers, or raising concerns through proper channels. If internal advocacy proves ineffective, external resources such as labor unions, employee advocacy groups, or legal protections may provide further support.

Reflection: Are Your Needs Being Fulfilled?

Workplace ethics can manifest in many ways—some obvious, others more subtle. You may not immediately recognize when your basic needs are not being met, but certain red flags should bring you to a deeper reflection. Consider the following questions to assess your employer's workplace ethics:

- *Do you feel that your hard work and contributions are ethically recognized and rewarded by your employer?*

- *Are you expected to regularly work beyond your agreed-upon hours without proper compensation or acknowledgment?*

- *Do you feel physically and psychologically safe in your workplace, free from harassment, discrimination, or unsafe conditions?*

- *Does your employer provide clear policies and resources to support workplace safety and mental health?*

- *Are promotions, raises, and growth opportunities ethically distributed, based on merit rather than favoritism?*

- *If you raise a workplace concern, does leadership or management take it seriously and respond with transparency and action?*

- *Does your company align with your values regarding ethical business practices, environmental responsibility, and social impact?*

- *Have you ever been asked to participate in, overlook, or ignore unethical behavior?*

- *Can you afford your basic needs without financial strain based on your current wages?*

- *If you needed to take time off for illness, family emergencies, or personal well-being, would your workplace support you without penalty?*

If you answered "no" to multiple questions, it may be time to reflect on whether your employer is meeting your fundamental needs. Recognizing ethical gaps is the first step toward advocating for change, whether through discussions with management, seeking external resources, or exploring alternative opportunities that align with your values and well-being.

Recognizing these workplace ethical issues is just the beginning. A truly ethical work environment is built on balance, a relationship where employers and employees contribute to and benefit from shared success. But what happens when this balance is disrupted? When the employer undermines the relationship with the employee through exploitative and abusive practices.

In the next chapter, you will take a broader look at the importance of a balanced relationship between employers and employees. You will explore how accountability and responsibility shape the modern workplace. Understanding this balance is key to navigating your career with confidence and ensuring that your work serves not just your employer, but also yourself.

Chapter 4:

Importance of a Balanced

Relationship

Michael always believed that hard work would earn him loyalty in return. When he landed a full-time job in a meat-packing company, he treated it like a long-term commitment. He showed up early, stayed late, and constantly proved his dedication. In the beginning, it felt like a strong partnership. His employer invested in training, provided ethical wages, and recognized his contributions. However, over time, things started to change. Expectations increased, but his pay remained stagnant. Overtime became mandatory, yet appreciation faded. When he raised concerns, he was met with dismissive responses. What once felt like a stable, mutual relationship now felt one-sided; he gave more than he was getting.

A job, much like a personal relationship, is built on an exchange of trust, effort, and respect. When both sides contribute equally, the relationship thrives, creating a stable and fulfilling work environment. But employees feel stuck, undervalued, and even trapped when one party dominates, whether through exploitative wages, unsafe conditions, or unrealistic demands.

In this chapter, you will explore the importance of a balanced relationship between employer and employee. Similar to personal relationships, balance is key to ensuring both parties benefit and grow. An ethical employment relationship is built on mutual respect, trust, and shared success. The relationship can become unstable when this balance is lost, leading to dissatisfaction, burnout, and exploitation. Throughout this chapter, we will also highlight the two key components to all healthy relationships, responsibility and accountability.

Comparing Employment to Relationships

Relationships, whether personal or professional, thrive on balance. In any partnership, both sides contribute effort, communication, and respect. When one party dominates or fails to uphold its responsibilities or works to avoid accountability, the relationship suffers. The same applies to the workplace. While some jobs promote stability and long-term growth, it is essential to remember that this is still a transactional relationship, which needs to be balanced. By drawing parallels between employment and different types of relationships, we can better understand what an ethical work environment looks like.

A Strong Marriage: The Ideal Employment Relationship

Imagine a long-term marriage where both partners respect and support each other. Each person brings value to the relationship, and when problems arise, they communicate and work through them together. Neither party takes the other for granted, and both are invested in each other's well-being and future. Both parties take responsibility for their personal actions and are open to their partners holding them accountable for those actions.

A healthy employment relationship mirrors this dynamic. Employment ethics establish a baseline that both parties can take responsibility for and be accountable to. When employers provide ethical wages, benefits, and a safe work environment, employees can bring their skills, effort, and dedication. When both the employer and employees are actively responsible and accountable, the organization can thrive, employees feel valued and secure, and employers gain a productive and loyal workforce. Companies that prioritize employee well-being through employment ethics are focused on creating more than success. Through their active responsibility and accountability, they are creating a legacy.

A One-Night Stand: Contractors, Part-Timers, and Gig Work

Not every relationship is built for the long haul. Some are short-term, serving a specific need without deep emotional investment. Think of a casual dating scenario where both parties know the relationship is temporary and based on convenience rather than long-term goals such as marriage.

This is similar to gig work and short-term employment. Many freelance or contract jobs operate on a transactional basis: workers complete a task, get paid, and move on. There is no expectation of long-term commitment or security. While this arrangement works well for those who value flexibility and independence, it lacks stability. Workers in these roles may have to constantly seek new opportunities, negotiate ethical compensation, and manage inconsistent income streams.

An Abusive Relationship: Exploitative Workplaces

In the worst-case scenario, a relationship becomes abusive. Although physical abuse in the workplace is rare, mental and emotional abuse is more common than people think. One of the main reasons for this is that a vital component of a successful relationship, balanced accountability, is instead very one-sided.

Consider an employee who works for long hours for minimal pay, fearing they will get fired if they speak up. Or a workplace where harassment and unsafe conditions are ignored, with management dismissing concerns. In these environments, employees may be uncertain of their rights or pressured to endure mistreatment for the sake of job security.

Recognizing these dynamics is essential. In a healthy personal relationship, both sides take an active role to ensure the personal well-being of the other—responsibility and accountability represent that active role. In an ethical workplace, both the employer (their representative) and the employee take an active role in ensuring their professional well-being.

Responsibility and accountability mean nothing if neither side of the relationship is dedicated to being *active* in the relationship's success. Understanding where your employment falls within these categories can help you determine whether you are in an ethical workplace or if it's time to seek something better. Imbalanced relationships can be harmful to all parties, and it is essential to understand when this is happening and what should be done in these cases.

How Imbalance Harms Employees and Employers

What is the cost of an abusive professional relationship? What happens when this balance is lost?

Employees experience dissatisfaction, burnout, and disengagement, while employers struggle with high turnover, reduced productivity, and long-term instability. Recognizing these effects is crucial to understanding why ethical employment practices benefit both workers and the company that relies on them.

Toll on Employees: Burnout, Job Dissatisfaction, and Turnover

When an employment relationship becomes one-sided, the first and most immediate impact is on the workers themselves. Employees who give their time, skills, and dedication but receive little support in return often experience burnout—physical, emotional, and mental exhaustion caused by prolonged workplace stress.

Think about an employee who is consistently expected to work late, take on additional responsibilities, and meet unrealistic performance targets without extra pay or recognition. Over time, this imbalance erodes motivation and well-being. A worker who once took pride in their role may start feeling undervalued, detached, and even resentful toward their employer. Job dissatisfaction then sets in, making it harder to stay engaged and productive.

As dissatisfaction grows, employees seek alternative opportunities. High turnover is a direct consequence of an imbalanced workplace. When workers feel overworked, unappreciated, and that they are working in unethical employment, they are more likely to leave in search of a more ethical workplace. The result? Companies lose experienced staff, which forces them to spend time and resources on hiring and training replacements, only for the cycle to repeat itself if systemic issues remain unaddressed.

James, a construction worker, prides himself on his strong work ethic and dedication to the job. His company, however, constantly demands overtime with little notice, often stretching shifts beyond 12 hours. He's expected to work weekends, even though he was originally hired for a standard schedule. When he asks about additional compensation, he's told, "This is how things are in the industry." Over time, exhaustion sets in, and injuries become more frequent among his crew. The stress of missing time with his family and the lack of recognition for his hard work led James to look for another job. Eventually, he leaves for a competitor that offers structured hours, proper overtime pay, and a focus on worker well-being. His former company, now struggling to retrain skilled laborers, finds itself unable to complete projects on time, causing delays and financial losses.

Toll on Employers: Reduced Productivity and Long-Term Instability

As you have seen, an imbalanced employment relationship doesn't just harm workers; it also weakens the companies that rely on them. Some employers mistakenly believe that squeezing as much labor as possible out of their employees maximizes efficiency. In reality, unethical employment practices tend to backfire, leading to decreased productivity, poor morale, and an unstable workforce.

When employees are overworked and undervalued, their performance suffers. Exhausted workers are more prone to errors, less engaged with their tasks, and less likely to contribute innovative ideas or creative solutions. A company that does not promote ethical employment practices may see short-term gains in output, but in the long run, a disengaged workforce leads to declining efficiency and profitability.

Additionally, high turnover rates create significant financial and operational burdens for employers. Constantly hiring and training new employees is costly, and frequent staff changes disrupt workflow and team dynamics. Beyond financial loss, a company with a reputation for unethical employment practices struggles to attract top talent. Skilled professionals are more likely to choose employers that offer ethical wages, job security, and a positive work culture.

A trucking company offers its drivers aggressive incentive programs to complete more deliveries in less time, pushing them to work long hours with minimal rest. While this initiative initially boosts revenue, it also leads to increased accidents, driver fatigue, and burnout. As safety concerns arise, experienced drivers leave for companies that respect federal driving regulations and prioritize rest periods. The company, now facing lawsuits and insurance hikes, is forced to reconsider its employment ethics and policies. By failing to balance productivity with ethical employee treatment, they ultimately hurt their bottom line and their reputation in the industry.

When an employment relationship is built on unethical practices, the consequences extend beyond the individual worker. Entire teams become demoralized, workplace culture suffers, and the company's overall success is put at risk. Therefore, a workplace cannot thrive if only one side benefits. A truly successful ethical employment relationship is one where employers and employees are invested in each other's success. Workers deserve ethical treatment, respect, and job security, while businesses need engaged, productive employees to achieve long-term growth.

So, what does a balanced employment relationship actually look like? Read on to explore the key elements of ethical employment practices, providing real-world examples of how companies and employees can create a mutually beneficial environment.

The Goal of Employment Ethics: A Balanced Relationship

Employment ethics represents the dynamic relationship between work ethic and employer ethics. It seeks to create a balanced employment relationship through both parties being active in maintaining the well-being of the other. Just like in any successful partnership, each side contributes and receives value in return. Workers bring in their skills, time, and dedication while employers provide an ethical workplace environment. When these elements are in place, job satisfaction increases, productivity improves, and businesses thrive. Let's look at some situations in which this standard is achieved.

Community: Earning a Living Without Financial Strain

A balanced workplace ensures that employees are, at a minimum, ethically compensated for their work. This means both receiving an hourly wage that allows them to live and participate in the surrounding community from which the employer draws their workforce. This should be able to be done through any full-time equivalent employment alone. In companies where wages are kept low, workers may be forced to work excessive overtime or seek additional jobs to make ends meet. This imbalance creates a financially insecure, overworked, and disengaged community. Ethical wages are not just a right; they are a necessity for any community to thrive.

Some electricians working in commercial construction are part of a group that negotiated strong wage agreements with their employers. They receive ethical pay that aligns with their living costs, ensuring they do not have to take on multiple jobs to support their families. In addition, their contracts include scheduled wage increases, paid time off, and health care benefits. Because of ethical employment practices, they can focus on their work without financial stress, leading to high job satisfaction and lower turnover rates.

Safety: Prioritizing Worker Well-Being

A balanced employment relationship also prioritizes safety. Employers who value their workforce invest in proper safety training, protective equipment, and enforceable policies that reduce workplace hazards. Workplaces that cut corners on safety measures act unethically by exposing their employees to unnecessary risks. Workers in high-risk industries deserve environments where their safety is a priority. Companies that fail to provide safe conditions will not only put their employees in danger but may also face legal issues, financial losses, and reputational damage.

At one metal fabrication plant, management recognized that frequent injuries were slowing down production and leading to high medical costs. Instead of pushing workers to keep up with unrealistic demands, they implemented a new safety training program, provided better protective gear, and encouraged workers to report hazards without fear of retaliation. Within a year, workplace injuries dropped significantly, morale improved, and production efficiency increased.

Respect: Treating Workers as Valued Professionals

One of the most overlooked but essential elements of a balanced workplace is respect. When employees are treated ethically, and with dignity, their morale and engagement increase. Ethical employers listen to worker concerns, involve employees in decision-making when possible, and maintain open lines of communication. A respectful workplace is one where employees feel heard, valued, and secure in their roles. When workers are treated as disposable or replaceable, morale declines, productivity drops, and turnover increases. Companies that respect their workforce create environments where employees are more likely to stay and take pride in their work.

One independent auto repair shop decided to change the common practice of failing to provide adequate career development opportunities and the lack of job security. Instead of treating mechanics as disposable workers, the owner implemented a structured training program that allowed employees to earn certifications at the company's expense. Additionally, the shop introduced a clear promotion path, ensuring that experienced mechanics could advance to higher-paying roles, such as lead technician or service manager. The shop also provided ethical commissioning, guaranteeing mechanics a steady income rather than relying only on fluctuating work orders. Employees who once saw auto repair as a temporary job now view it as a long-term career. As a result, customer service improved, turnover decreased, and the business grew.

Accountability: Holding Employers to Ethical Standards

In a balanced workplace, all parties are held accountable for their responsibilities. This means workers are expected to efficiently perform their duties, while management ensures policies are applied consistently and ethically. A lack of accountability leads to frustration, disengagement, and a lack of trust between employers and employees. A balanced workplace ensures that policy applies equally to all, rewarding hard work and ethically addressing issues.

A construction firm was experiencing favoritism in promotions, where certain employees received career advancement opportunities regardless of experience. Recognizing this issue, the company implemented a transparent promotion system, ensuring that training, certifications, and performance reviews determined career progression. Employees now had a clear growth path based on merit, leading to a more motivated workforce and a stronger sense of ethical treatment within the company.

When ethical wages, safe conditions, respect, and accountability are present in the workplace, employees feel valued, motivated, and secure in their roles. Companies that implement ethical employment practices benefit from lower turnover, higher productivity, and a positive reputation in their industry. If workers recognize that their current job lacks these essential elements and their advocacy for change is ignored, either their work ethic will suffer, or they will seek out a more ethical workplace.

Reflection: How Do You Evaluate Your Work Relationship?

A balanced work relationship is built on different ethical employment practices. With this in mind, the question is: Does your current job measure up? Take a moment to reflect on your own experience by answering the following questions. Your responses will help you determine whether your employment relationship is balanced—or if it is time to take action.

- *Do you feel that your employer values your contribution and recognizes your hard work?*

- *Are you ethically compensated for your skills, experience, and the effort you put into the job?*

- *Does your workplace provide a safe and healthy environment?*

- *Are you able to maintain a work–life balance, or are you regularly expected to sacrifice your personal time?*

- *When concerns arise, do you feel comfortable bringing them up to management or HR without fear of retaliation?*

- *Are opportunities for raises, promotions, and career growth transparent and based on merit?*

- *Does your company actively invest in employee well-being, training, or professional development?*

- *Are workplace policies and expectations applied consistently to all employees?*

- *If you had the choice, would you recommend your job to a friend or family member?*

If you answered "no" to multiple questions, your workplace may not be providing the balance and ethical conditions needed for a healthy employment relationship. While some issues can be addressed through open communication and advocacy, others may require considering alternative employment opportunities. The most important step is recognizing when an imbalance exists; only then can you begin taking action to create a better work experience for yourself.

Remember: A strong work ethic is built on strong employer ethics. Organizations with a reputation for poor employment ethics will be viewed as the employer of last resort by the workforce within their community. They will be known for corrupting and stifling the work ethic of their staff. Employers with low employer ethics justify the low work ethic of their employees through their disregard for the needs of their employees. Finally, now that you have seen how responsibility and accountability matter, it is time to explore how Maslowian principles affect employer ethics and the employee–employer relationship.

Chapter 5:

A Safe and Secure

Workplace

Every worker has the right to feel safe in their job. Whether operating on heavy machinery, working in a factory, taking care of a patient, driving a truck, or serving coffee, safety should never be left to chance. Over time, workplace safety laws have been created to ensure that employees are protected from harm, unethical treatment, and hazardous working conditions. However, the responsibility of workplace safety does not solely rest on regulations; employer ethics require the employer to actively ensure that their standards create a safe and secure work environment to the reasonable best of their ability.

Safety needs extend beyond physical protection; they also include job security, workplace safety, and psychological well-being. Ethical workplaces go beyond just meeting the minimum legal requirements—they take proactive steps to ensure employee health and stability. This includes providing clear safety protocols, preventing workplace harassment, and ensuring job security through ethical employment practices.

Although the focus here is on a physically safe and secure environment, it also goes beyond that. It is essential to remember that the financial stability of an employee ensures that they can meet all of their personal and familial needs. This is the primary reason most employees work for an employer. Due to that, job security is also a vital and often-overlooked aspect of a safe and secure workplace, which we get into in a later chapter.

Despite legal protections, some companies still engage in unethical practices that create instability and anxiety in their employees. Mass layoffs without notice, lack of safety equipment, and refusal to support the physical and mental well-being of its workforce can all lead to an unsafe and stressful work environment. Conversely, ethical employers take a more responsible approach. They prioritize transparent communication, provide severance packages when necessary, and offer mental health support to create a psychologically and physically secure workplace.

Understand that being an ethical employer means the employer is actively working to go above and beyond the legal minimum. History is filled with countless stories of employers constantly fighting against the workforce's demand for a safe and secure workspace. What follows is just a handful of examples.

Historical Employer Neglect

Before the establishment of workplace safety regulations in the US, many industries operated with little to no regard for employee well-being. Factories, mines, and construction sites prioritized productivity and profit over safety, leading to numerous injuries and fatalities. Workers, many of whom were women and children, were subjected to dangerous machinery, toxic environments, and extensive hours without protection. It was only after repeated disasters and public outcry that significant reforms took place. From the deadly consequences of the Industrial Revolution to workplace tragedies, history has shown that unchecked employer negligence leads to catastrophic results.

Industrial Revolution and the Rise of Dangerous Workplaces

The Industrial Revolution transformed the U.S. economy for the better, but at the same time, it also created dangerous working conditions. The rapid expansion of factories led to long hours, poor ventilation, and the introduction of hazardous working machinery. The more these industries grew, the workplaces became less safe, with little to no concern for worker safety. Children worked in textile and coal mines, often performing dangerous tasks for low wages.

In textile factories, unguarded machines held the danger of catching a worker's clothing, pulling them into deadly gear. In coal mines, workers faced frequent collapses and methane explosions, both of which killed thousands of employees every year. Finally, in steel mills and railroad construction, workers had to face extreme heat, heavy materials, and extensive shifts, leaving them physically exhausted and prone to accidents.

As public awareness of these dangers grew, workplace injuries and hazards gained visibility. The labor movement and progressive politicians pushed for reforms, eventually leading to the establishment of workplace safety laws. However, it took several high-profile tragedies before the real change occurred.

Triangle Shirtwaist Factory Fire (1911)

One of the most well-known workplace disasters in U.S. history happened in New York: the Triangle Shirtwaist Factory fire. At the time, the accident exposed the horrifying conditions of garment workers. The factory employed mostly young immigrant women who worked long hours in a cramped space filled with flammable fabric.

On March 25, 1911, a fire broke out on the upper floors of the building where the factory stood. Many workers couldn't escape since management had locked the doors to prevent unauthorized breaks. As flames spread, workers had no choice but to jump from windows or be consumed by the fire. Over 100 people lost their lives in the tragic accident, leading to public outrage (The Editors of Encyclopædia Britannica,

2025b). The fire led to a push for labor reforms, including safety fire laws, workplace exit regulations, and building codes, establishing modern fire safety standards.

Hawks Nest Tunnel Disaster (1927–1932)

During the construction of the Hawks Nest Tunnel in West Virginia, hundreds of workers were exposed to silica dust while drilling through rock. Most of these were African-American migrant workers who worked long hours in the tunnel. Despite the well-known dangers of silica exposure, those workers were not provided with protective equipment (such as masks) or ventilation.

As a result, over 1,000 individuals developed silicosis, a fatal lung disease, and more than 700 died from complications. Others developed symptoms throughout time and had to face serious health consequences, ultimately leading to death. Many of these deaths would have been preventable had the company implemented basic dust control measures. This case contributed to later workplace health regulations, ensuring that companies are accountable for protecting workers from long-term exposure to harmful substances.

Monongah Mining Disaster (1907)

Coal mining was one of the most dangerous professions in the early 20th century. Workers were exposed to frequent cave-ins, explosions, and gas poisoning. On December 6, 1907, the Monongah Mine in West Virginia had one of the deadliest mining accidents in U.S. history, when an underground explosion killed more than 350 workers.

Despite the issues, mine owners resisted safety improvements because accidents were seen as part of the job. However, later investigations revealed that a lack of ventilation, poor infrastructure, and failure to follow safety protocols led to the explosion. The disaster finally pushed lawmakers to establish the Bureau of Mines, the first government agency dedicated to mine safety. Its implementation led to stricter mine ventilation laws, safety inspection protocols, and improved training for miners, bringing significant change to the job.

Willow Island Disaster (1978)

The construction industry has always been high-risk, but the collapse of the Willow Island cooling tower in West Virginia is still one of the worst accidents in history. During the construction of a power plant cooling tower, scaffolding and concrete supports failed, causing 51 workers to fall to their deaths. Investigations later found that improper safety inspections, rushed work schedules, and poor construction practices led to the catastrophe. This tragedy reinforced the need for strict workplace safety enforcement in construction, leading to stronger fall protection laws, equipment testing requirements, and training programs.

The Path to Reform

Each of these disasters shares a common theme: employers who ignored safety in favor of profit, leading to preventable loss of life. Most major workplace safety regulations are the result of employer ethics failures, often multiple times. The cost of these failures is paid for primarily by the employees' health and well-being. It was only from the hard work of the workforce, allied unions, and activists that these, and many other organizations, are held accountable, and the regulations enacted. Some of the key reforms resulting from these tragedies include

- fire safety laws (after the Triangle Shirtwaist Factory fire)

- mine safety regulations (after the Monongah mining disaster)

- occupational disease protection (after the Hawks Nest Tunnel disaster)

- construction safety standards (after the Willow Island collapse)

- creation of the Occupational Safety and Health Administration (OSHA) (1970) to enforce nationwide workplace safety laws

Despite these improvements, workplace safety is still a concern today. Modern challenges come from three areas: gig work, advanced automation, and political pressures. In the next section, you will continue to explore the agencies responsible for enforcing workplace safety laws and how they continue to shape safer work environments for employees across industries.

Creation of Worker Safety Agencies

The workplace disasters and tragedies of the past made it clear that leaving worker safety to employers' discretion was not enough. The widespread negligence highlighted the urgent need for government oversight. As a result, safety agencies were established worldwide to enforce regulations, conduct inspections, and hold companies accountable for maintaining safe work environments.

Blue-collar workers often face the highest risks due to the physical nature of their jobs, so these agencies play a critical role in ensuring their well-being. While workplace safety organizations exist in nearly every country, five major agencies have set global standards and continue to shape workplace protections today.

Occupational Safety and Health Administration (US)

The OSHA was established in 1970 under the Occupational Safety and Health Act to address the growing concerns about workplace injuries and fatalities. OSHA enforces safety regulations across industries, with a strong focus on blue-collar sectors such as construction, manufacturing, warehousing, and transportation. The standard carries out regular inspections and provides whistleblower protections for workers who report unsafe conditions.

In industries where cutting corners on safety is common, OSHA plays an essential role in ensuring employers follow safety guidelines. Key protection for workers in OSHA include

- fall protection regulations for construction workers on scaffolding or rooftops.

- machine guarding standards for factory workers operating heavy machinery.

- hazard communication rules to protect workers handling toxic materials.

- noise and respiratory protection in high-risk environments such as mining and metalworking.

- personal protective equipment requirements for industries like welding and lodging.

Health and Safety Executive (UK)

The Health and Safety Executive (HSE) was created in 1974 under the Health and Safety at Work Act in the UK. Similar to OSHA, HSE enforces regulations, conducts workplace inspections, and ensures that companies provide a safe working environment. HSE is especially strict in employer liability, ensuring that companies cannot avoid responsibility for workplace injuries. The organization has set the foundation for many European workplace safety laws and continues to be a model for labor protection worldwide.

Some of the protections included in the HSE encompass

- construction site safety standards that require scaffolding inspections and fall protection.

- risk assessment requirements to identify and minimize workplace hazards.

- manual handling regulations to prevent injuries from lifting heavy objects.

- enforcement of asbestos exposure rules, protecting construction and demolition workers.

- agricultural safety regulations that address risks for farm and field workers.

German Social Accident Insurance (Germany)

Germany has one of the world's most advanced protection systems, especially due to the German Social Accident Insurance (DGUV). Founded in 1884, it is one of the oldest workplace safety organizations in the world. DGUV operates under a system where employees pay into accident insurance funds, which provide compensation to injured workers and enforce safety measures. What makes the DGUV unique is its proactive approach: Instead of only reacting to accidents, it emphasizes prevention by requiring industries to adopt safety measures before workers are harmed.

This system has significantly reduced workplace fatalities in Germany's heavy industries by enforcing protections such as

- strong workplace accident compensation programs, ensuring injured workers receive medical care and financial support.

- extensive workplace training programs to prevent injuries before they happen.

- strict equipment safety standards in construction, manufacturing, and logistics industries.

- comprehensive insurance coverage for workplace injuries and illnesses.

Safe Work Australia (Australia)

Australia's Safe Work Australia was established in 2008 and played a major part in improving worker safety through a national approach. Unlike OSHA or HSE, which have direct enforcement powers, Safe Work Australia develops policies and safety codes that each Australian state enforces independently. Safe Work Australia's influence extends beyond just national regulations; it also sets global benchmarks in industries such as mining and construction, where the country has some of the highest safety standards worldwide.

Key protections for blue-collar workers in Safe Work Australia include

- construction safety policies that address high-risk jobs like roofing, demolition, and excavation.

- mining regulations to protect workers from toxic exposure, explosions, and collapses.

- occupational disease monitoring to ensure that long-term health risks, such as mesothelioma from asbestos exposure, are tracked.

- heavy vehicle safety programs, aimed at truck drivers facing long shifts and fatigue-related accidents.

International Organization for Standardization (Global)

Unlike the other organizations you saw before, the International Organization for Standardization (ISO) does not enforce laws but instead creates international safety standards that companies voluntarily follow. These standards are widely adopted by businesses looking to improve workplace safety beyond their national requirements. ISO is particularly useful for multinational companies and industries that operate across borders, ensuring that safety standards remain consistent worldwide.

Safety standards developed by ISO companies usually include the following:

- **ISO 45001:** Occupational health and safety management system; a framework for improving workplace safety.

- **ISO 14001:** Environmental management standards that protect workers from hazardous waste exposure.

- **ISO 9001:** Quality management standards that prevent defective and dangerous equipment use.

Other Organizations

In addition to these major agencies, several industry-specific organizations help protect workers in high-risk jobs:

- **Mine Safety and Health Administration (MSHA) (US):** Focused on coal, metal, and nonmetal mining safety.

- **Federal Motor Carrier Safety Administration (FMCSA) (US):** Regulates truck driver safety and working hours.

- **National Institute for Occupational Safety and Health (NIOSH) (US):** researches workplace health risks and solutions.

- **United Steelworkers (USW) (international):** Advocates for industrial and factory worker protections.

Each of these agencies plays a role in ensuring that blue-collar workers in specific fields receive the necessary protection from workplace hazards. Thanks to these organizations' efforts, workplace injuries and fatalities have steadily declined over the past century. However, modern challenges such as gig work, automation, and mental health concerns require continuous adaptation of safety regulations.

Understanding the role of safety agencies is essential for workers in any industry. Whether you are in construction, manufacturing, transportation, or other blue-collar activities, these agencies set the standards that protect you every day. At the same time, the work is not yet done. As you move on, you will explore current challenges and gaps in workplace safety, including the impact of modern labor trends on worker protection.

Current Issues and Gaps

The world of work has drastically changed in the 21st century. Employers have increased their dependency on independent contractors and part-time or "gig" workers, as well as outsourcing human resources and hiring responsibilities. This has been done to create an illusion of decreasing costs, but at the same time, it has made it harder for employees to hold employers accountable for unethical practices. For example, gig workers such as rideshare drivers, food delivery couriers, warehouse packers, and freelance laborers lack many of the legal protections that traditional employees receive.

This present situation happens mainly due to employers taking advantage of governments' slow response to changes and the amount of money many employers invest in advocacy on their behalf to maintain an outdated status quo that they can abuse. While some countries are responding to these new changes in the economy, there are still challenges that need to be addressed to ensure these individuals are protected from workplace hazards.

The Safety Challenges of Gig Work

- **No employer-provided safety equipment:** Unlike traditional jobs, gig workers are often responsible for their own protective gear, such as helmets, gloves, and masks, even when working in hazardous conditions.

- **Lack of workers' compensation:** If a gig worker is injured on the job, they often do not qualify for workers' compensation benefits since they are not considered formal employees.

- **Unstable work schedules and fatigue risks:** Many gig workers work long and unpredictable hours to make ends meet, increasing the risk of fatigue-related accidents.

- **No whistleblower protections:** Gig workers who report unsafe conditions have little recourse if a company chooses to deactivate or ban them from the platform.

Some governments are beginning to address these issues. In California, the 2019 AB5 law attempted to reclassify certain gig workers as employees, requiring companies like Uber and Lyft to provide benefits. However, these efforts have faced pushback, and legal battles continue. In contrast, Europe has taken strong steps, with the EY Platform Work Directive pushing for gig worker protections such as minimum wages, insurance, and legal representation. While several steps are being taken to ensure these workers are protected, gig workers in the US still remain largely unprotected, and federal legislation is still lagging behind the realities of modern labor.

Automation and Workplace Safety Risks

While automation is often seen as a way to reduce workplace injuries by replacing human labor with machines, it has also introduced new safety concerns for workers who interact with automated systems. In some industries, automated machinery and AI-driven processes are becoming more common. Although this may seem like a positive effort, without proper oversight, they pose serious risks. Some of these include

- **Increased risk of machine-related injuries:** Workers who operate automated forklifts, robotic arms, and self-driving vehicles face an increased risk of accidental collisions, malfunctions, or entrapments.

- **Job displacement and the rise of temporary work:** Although the fear of complete replacement of the human workforce by automation has been disproven, the rise of supplemental or temporary workforces, combined with a drastic decrease in hiring regular full-time employees, has been well documented.

- **Lack of regulation for AI-driven equipment:** Unlike traditional machinery, AI-controlled robots and self-operating vehicles have little government oversight, leading to unclear liability when accidents occur.

- **Ergonomic risks from new technology:** As automation reduces physical labor, some workers are forced into repetitive and high-speed tasks, leading to an increase in body movement disorders.

OSHA has started being more proactive, updating its regulations to include robotic safety guidelines, but enforcement remains weak. Germany's DGUV has been more proactive, requiring human oversight of AI-controlled systems and mandating emergency shutoff features in automated warehouses. However, workplace automation laws in most countries remain outdated, creating a gray area where companies can introduce automation without proper safety measures. Without stronger international safety standards, automation will continue to increase productivity at the cost of worker safety.

Mental Health and Workplace Safety: The Overlooked Crisis

For decades, workplace safety regulations focused primarily on physical hazards, such as falls, machinery accidents, and toxic exposure. Today, other issues, especially mental health risks—including stress, burnout, and workplace harassment—are now recognized as serious threats to worker well-being. Examples of these risks include

- **Workplace stress and burnout:** High workloads, unrealistic productivity expectations, and poor work–life balance are leading to record levels of stress-related illnesses.

- **Lack of employer mental health support:** Many companies do not provide mental health resources, leaving workers to handle job-related stress on their own.

- **Suicide and workplace trauma:** High-stress industries such as construction, emergency response, law enforcement, and trucking have some of the highest suicide rates, yet few employers have prevention programs in place.

In 2021, the US introduced workplace mental health guidelines under OSHA's General Duty Clause, urging employers to address stress and burnout. Despite being created, these guidelines are not legally enforceable. On the other hand, the UK's HSE has been more proactive, requiring companies to assess mental health risks as part of their overall workplace safety policies. In Asia, Japan introduced the *karoshi* (death from overwork) laws, capping overtime hours to prevent excessive work-related stress.

Despite these efforts, many countries still treat mental health as a secondary issue, and enforcement remains weak. More laws are needed to ensure that mental well-being is treated with the same level of importance as physical safety.

Reflection: Do You Work in a Safe and Secure Environment?

Workplace safety goes beyond avoiding accidents; it also includes job security, mental well-being, and ethical treatment. While regulations exist to protect workers, not all employers enforce them properly. Take a moment to reflect upon your work environment by answering these questions, applicable across different industries, from truck workers and warehouse workers to restaurant servers and health care professionals:

- *Are you provided with proper safety equipment and training relevant to your job (e.g., gloves, harnesses, masks, or lifting techniques)?*

- *Does your employer have a clear emergency response plan in case of fires, medical emergencies, or workplace violence?*

- *Do you feel pressured to work through illness, injury, or extreme fatigue due to fear of job loss or disciplinary action?*

- *Are staffing levels adequate to ensure safety, or does short-staffing regularly create hazardous conditions (e.g., nurses handling too many patients, truckers pushed to drive without rest, or kitchen staff working in unsafe heat conditions)?*

- *Do you or your coworkers regularly experience verbal abuse, harassment, or discrimination without proper action being taken?*

- *Is your employer transparent about workplace hazards, or do they downplay risks to avoid liability?*

- *Do you feel comfortable reporting usage conditions without fear of retaliation or job loss?*

- *Are breaks and rest periods enforced, or are you expected to push through exhaustion to meet unrealistic productivity demands?*

- *Does your job provide mental health resources or support systems to handle stress, trauma, or workplace-related anxiety?*

- *If an injury were to occur on the job, do you trust that your employer would handle it ethically, covering medical expenses and ensuring you have time to recover?*

If you answered "no" to multiple questions, your workplace may not be prioritizing safety and well-being. Recognizing these issues is the first step toward advocating for change, and if this does not work, seeking alternative employment where safety is taken seriously should be considered.

A safe and secure workplace is only one piece of ethical employment. Even when physical safety is prioritized, workers can still face discrimination, bias, and unethical treatment that threaten their well-being and job security. Throughout history, employers have abused their power through racism, sexism, ableism, xenophobia, and other forms of discrimination, creating hostile work environments that exclude and exploit certain groups.

In the next chapter, you will explore what an accountable professional relationship looks like and how systemic biases have shaped workplace culture. From historical injustices to modern workplace discrimination, we will examine the role of legal protections, company policies, and personal advocacy in ensuring that every worker is treated ethically and respectfully. Understanding these issues is critical in building a workplace where all employees have an equal opportunity to thrive.

Chapter 6:

An Accountable

Professional Relationship

The transactional nature of employment ethics means that things like friendships and respect, both aspects of higher needs according to Maslow, are not considered. Instead, employment ethics demands, at a minimum, a professional relationship between the employer and the employee. The employee is hired to do a job, and the employer is responsible for the work environment in which the employee does that job. Favoritism, nepotism, discriminatory practices, and harassment, for either party, undermine the professional work environment.

These practices threaten the employee's safety and security, hindering their ability to do their job and meet their needs through employment. The employer is ultimately responsible for the professional environment through policy establishment and accountable relationship maintenance. Ethical lapses, especially at the management level, can lead to widespread disillusionment and disengagement among employees.

One of the many ways employers work to meet their legal and ethical demands for developing a professional environment is through what has become known as diversity, equity, inclusion, and access (DEIA) initiatives. These encompass everything from hiring and promotion practices to the inclusion of handicap stalls in bathrooms, nonsegregated drinking fountains, and sexual harassment protections. DEIA policies demand, at a minimum, a professional relationship between the employer and current and potential employees so they can all be successful. An additional benefit of DEIA practices is that they reflect an evolving understanding of how diversity strengthens workplace relationships and enhances business performance.

Examples of unethical workplace applications include favoritism, inconsistent disciplinary actions, and a lack of transparency in promotions. These practices can erode trust, and employment ethics require consistent accountability, open communication, and a commitment to ethical standards. This also extends to performance evaluations, which should ensure employees receive constructive feedback based on merit rather than personal bias.

Different studies have been carried out to show that diverse teams drive innovation, improve problem-solving, and increase profitability. Employers that actively pursue DEIA principles have higher employee satisfaction, better decision-making, and a more inclusive culture that fosters collaboration. However, the effectiveness of these programs depends on whether they are genuinely integrated into company policies or merely used as performative branding. Employees can quickly tell the difference between a company that values DEIA and one that is trying to gain favor without any real accountability. Understanding these challenges is key to ensuring that all workers are evaluated based on merit, skill, and contribution rather than outdated workplace norms.

Workplace Discrimination and Abuse

Despite modern efforts to promote DEIA, workplace discrimination remains a persistent issue. Throughout history, employees have been mistreated based on race, gender, disability, sexual orientation, and nationality. It was not uncommon for these groups to be denied opportunities, ethical wages, or even basic respect. While laws have been introduced to combat these injustices, the fight for equitable and ethical workplaces is ongoing.

Racism in the Workplace: The Pullman Porters

In the late 19th and 20th centuries, one of the most prestigious jobs available to Black men was working as a Pullman Porter on luxury railway, or Palace, cars. While these jobs provided employment opportunities for African Americans after slavery, the reality of the work was far from glamorous: They were underpaid, overworked, and subject to racial discrimination. They were expected to work long hours without rest, endure demeaning treatment from passengers, and rely on tips instead of ethical wages. Despite their hard work, they were rarely promoted, and their complaints about working conditions were ignored.

In 1925, the Brotherhood of Sleeping Car Porters was founded. It was the first Black-led labor union in the US and fought for better wages, reduced working hours, and respect on the job. This led to securing improvements that benefited future generations of Black workers. Their efforts paved the way for civil rights advocacy in the labor movement and demonstrated the power of collective action in combating workplace racism.

Sexism and the Fight for Equal Pay: The Radium Girls

In the early 20th century, thousands of women were hired to paint watch dials with radium-based luminous paint. The job required delicate handwork, and these women, also known as Radium Girls, were encouraged to lick their paintbrushes to keep the tips fine, leading them to ingest the deadly radioactive material. The companies that employed them denied wrongdoing, despite the evidence that these women were suffering from severe symptoms. Some of these included radiation poisoning, losing teeth, developing tumors, and dying prematurely.

At the same time, male scientists and supervisors who handled the radium were given protective gear, highlighting the general negligence in workplace safety. When the women sued, they faced corporate denial and legal obstacles. However, their persistence led to an out-of-court settlement in 1928. Later in 1970, they participated in one of the most significant workplace reforms in U.S. history.

Ableism In Employment: Workplace Accessibility

In the past, people with disabilities were excluded from the workforce, either by outright discrimination or by workplaces failing to provide the necessary accommodations. One significant moment in the fight for disability rights happened in the 1970s when disabled activists staged sit-ins at federal buildings. Their main demand was the enforcement of Section 504 of the Rehabilitation Act, which prohibited discrimination based on disability for federal-funded programs.

Until then, many workplaces, public buildings, and transportation systems were inaccessible to the disabled. Even with the law increasing protections and ensuring accessibility, such as the Americans with Disabilities Act of 1990, workplace discrimination continues. Many companies still fail to provide reasonable accommodations, such as wheelchair-accessible facilities or adaptive technology for the visually impaired.

Fighting Against Homophobia: The Case of LGBTQ+ Workers

Before the landmark Supreme Court Ruling in 2020 that made it illegal to fire someone for being LGBTQ+, workers who identified as such faced widespread discrimination with little protection. These employees were granted federal protection against gender identity or sexual orientation, ensuring ethical opportunities. Before, many were fired, harassed, or even denied promotions due to their identities.

One notable case was Jameka Evans, a hospital security guard in Georgia who was fired in 2013 for not conforming to gender norms. The employer claimed she did not behave or present herself in a womanly manner. Evans was also a lesbian, which increased the discrimination, leading to legal battles that eventually led to stronger workplace protections for LGBTQ+ workers.

Xenophobia and Workplace Discrimination: Immigrant Exploitation

Throughout history, immigrant workers faced low wages, dangerous working conditions, and discrimination. In the US, this was particularly evident in the 1900s, when Irish, Chinese, and Mexican workers were given the most physically demanding and unsafe jobs in industries like railroad construction, agriculture, and factories. In more recent years, migrant farmworkers, who often do not have legal documentation, face exploitation, wage theft, and unsafe working conditions.

Even in high-skilled industries, immigrants often face workplace discrimination. Many employers prefer US-born applicants or underpay skilled foreign workers when compared to their counterparts. Despite many economies depending on the immigrant workforce, bias and xenophobia continue to create barriers to ethical employment. In 2022, the Department of Labor found that many U.S. farms violated labor laws, underpaying workers and failing to provide safe housing, leading employers to pay millions in back wages.

These stories reflect an employer's failure to uphold basic ethical standards. In most cases, without government intervention, workplace discrimination would likely continue unchecked. Holding companies accountable is the only time change happens, such as with the passage of civil rights laws, equal pay acts, and antidiscrimination policies. These measures have proven to be essential in improving workplace conditions for workers.

Government Intervention

Workers have fought tirelessly for their right to ethical treatment throughout time, demanding their right to ethical treatment, equal opportunities, and safe workplaces. Discrimination and unethical labor practices persist without government intervention, showcasing the importance of regulatory measures. To combat these injustices, many governments worldwide have implemented laws, policies, and enforcement agencies aimed at promoting workplace diversity and inclusion. Read on to learn more about a few of these initiatives.

Equal Employment Opportunity Commission (US)

In the US, one of the most influential bodies in workplace equality is the Equal Employment Opportunity Commission (EEOC). Established in 1965, the EEOC was created as a part of the Civil Rights Act of 1964 to enforce federal laws prohibiting workplace discrimination based on race, color, religion, sex, or national origin. Over the decades, its scope has expanded to include protections against ageism, disability discrimination, and LGBTQ+ workplace rights. Some of the impacts of the EEOC include

- enforcing antidiscrimination laws so that employers cannot make hiring, firing, or promotion decisions based on protected characteristics such as race, gender, and disability.

- investigating workplace discrimination complaints for any worker who feels discriminated against, potentially leading to investigating, mediating, or taking legal action.

- expanding legal practices, including establishing cases that have led to landmark Supreme Court rulings, such as the 2020 Bostock v. Clayton County decision, which affirmed that LGBTQ+ workers are protected from discrimination under Title VII of the Civil Rights Act.

Despite its progress, the EEOC faces challenges in enforcement. Many cases take years to resolve, and some employers continue discriminatory practices despite legal protections. Stronger penalties and quicker case resolutions remain key areas for improvement.

Equality Act (UK)

The UK Equality Act of 2010 is one of the most comprehensive antidiscrimination laws in the world. It replaced previous antidiscrimination laws with a single, unified framework covering race, gender, disability, age, religion, sexual orientation, and pregnancy and maternity protections. This law has strengthened workplace diversity in the UK, including actions such as

- worker protection from unethical treatment, where all employers must treat employees ethically in hiring, pay, promotions, and working conditions.

- mandating equal pay where men and women must be paid the same for the same work.

- introducing the concept of protected characteristics, where workers cannot be discriminated against based on specific personal traits.

- covering harassment and victimization so that employees are protected from workplace bullying related to their identity.

While this law presents significant advances in workplace diversity, pay gaps and underrepresentation of minorities in leadership roles remain important concerns. Critics argue that more proactive enforcement and greater penalties for noncompliance are needed.

Canadian Human Rights Commission

The Canadian Human Rights Commission (CHRC) was created in 1977 to uphold the Canadian Human Rights Act, which prohibits workplace discrimination based on race, age, gender, disability, and other protected characteristics. In addition to protecting employees from discrimination and harassment, the CHRC actively promotes workplace diversity and inclusion through initiatives such as

- the Employment Equity Act of 1986, which requires large employers to hire and promote diverse candidates, including Indigenous people, women, disabled individuals, and visible minorities.

- the Pay Equity Legislation, which ensures that women receive equal pay for work of equal value.

- accessibility laws that employers must follow to provide reasonable accommodations for disabled workers.

Despite the progress, Indigenous and Black Canadians continue to face barriers to employment, and many employers fail to meet employment equity targets. This situation has led to calls from the population for stronger penalties, and more proactive diversity policies are increasing.

European Equality Bodies

Across Europe, workplace equality is enforced through different national agencies and EU-wide policies. Some of the most notable include

- **European Union antidiscrimination laws:** The E.U. Employment Equality Directive of 2000 prohibits workplace discrimination based on religion, disability, age, or sexual orientation across all E.U. countries. Additionally, the Gender Equality Directive of 2006 enforces equal pay and maternity protections.

- **Germany DGUV:** Germany enforces workplace equality through its labor laws and antidiscrimination agencies, including the General Equal Treatment Act of 2006. In it, employers must ensure a discrimination-free workplace with violations leading to legal penalties. The DGUV also monitors employer compliance with antidiscrimination standards.

- **French High Authority for the Fight Against Discrimination for Equality (HALDE):** The HALDE was established in 2004 to investigate workplace discrimination complaints and ensure that hiring, promotions, and workplace policies comply with equality laws.

Although European countries have made significant progress, disparities remain. Even with legal protections, companies continue to exploit loopholes, employees still face bias, and some workplaces resist change. Some issues, including retaliation against employees who report discrimination, still occur, and it is essential for there to be a more proactive approach to the matter. This is why ongoing government oversight and stronger enforcement of workplace protections are necessary to create truly equitable and ethical professional relationships.

Challenges and Modern Issues

Despite the implementation of laws and corporate diversity initiatives, many employees still face systemic challenges in the workplace. These challenges, such as wage gaps, workplace harassment, and discrimination in hiring and promotion, persist in many industries. More often than not, they are masked by corporate policies that appear ethical on the surface but fail in practice. Understanding how these issues manifest and how employers sometimes disguise them is crucial in recognizing and addressing workplace inequalities.

Wage Gaps

The wage gap remains a major issue, particularly affecting women, racial minorities, and disabled workers. While companies often claim to offer "equal pay for equal work," loopholes and hidden pay structures allow disparities to continue. In many cases, women still earn less than men, just as disabled workers earn less than their able-bodied counterparts, and homosexual individuals receive lower wages than heterosexuals. Employers disguise these practices in pay disparities with actions such as

- **Secrecy in salaries:** Many companies discourage employees from discussing their salaries, making it difficult to detect pay disparities.

- **Merit-based raises that favor certain groups:** Some companies claim that pay differences are based on performance rather than gender or race, although it has been shown that biases play a role in performance evaluations.

- **Unequal starting salaries:** Women and minorities are often offered lower initial salaries, which affects long-term earnings. Since raises are typically percentage-based, an unethical starting salary results in a continued wage gap.

- **Lack of pay transparency:** Many companies refuse to publicly disclose salary bands, making it impossible for employees to compare wages.

Workplace Harassment

Although several countries offer legal protections, workplace harassment, including sexual harassment, bullying, and microaggressions, remains a serious issue. Victims are usually targeted by inappropriate comments, unwanted advances, and even assaults. At the same time, employees who speak up about unethical practices often experience demotions, terminations, or even microaggressions. It is not uncommon for minority employees to be excluded from conversations or to have their qualifications questioned, creating a hostile work environment. This harassment is disguised with actions that include, but are not limited to

- **"Zero tolerance" policies that lack enforcement:** Many companies claim to have strict harassment policies but fail to act when complaints are made.

- **Forcing employees into confidential agreements (nondisclosure agreements):** Some companies use nondisclosure agreements to prevent employees from publicly disclosing harassment occurrences.

- **HR bias toward the company:** Many employees report harassment to HR, only to find that they prioritize company interests rather than protecting the victim.

- **Retaliation against victims:** It has been shown that employees who report harassment face some form of retaliation, including being denied promotions or even fired.

Discrimination in Hiring and Promotions

While many employers claim to value diversity, hiring and promotion discrimination remain widespread issues. Even when companies appear diverse at entry-level positions, leadership remains overwhelmingly white, male, and able-bodied. Candidates from minority groups usually receive fewer callbacks, women are not promoted to leadership positions, and conservative industries lack LGBTQ+ diversity. These biases are usually disguised with actions such as

- **Diversity quotas that lack substance:** Some companies hire diverse candidates to meet quotas but fail to support their advancement.

- **"Cultural fit" as a hiring excuse:** Many hiring managers reject minority candidates by claiming they don't fit with company culture, which is often code for bias.

- **Subjective promotion criteria:** Performance evaluations tend to favor dominant groups through unconscious bias, allowing men and white employees to advance more easily.

- **Unpaid internships and exclusionary networks:** Many minority and low-income candidates cannot afford unpaid internships, limiting access to career-advancing opportunities.

As you reflect on these challenges, it becomes clear that workplace equality requires more than just policies; it demands accountability. In the next section, you will be able to reflect on whether your current employer upholds their commitment to DEIA. These questions will help you identify and ensure these principles are not just words but also actions that impact corporate culture.

Reflection Section: Is Your Workplace Truly Inclusive?

Creating an ethical workplace goes beyond compliance with laws. It requires a culture of accountability and respect for all employees. Take a moment to evaluate your workplace using the following questions. These will help assess whether your company actively fosters a DEIA environment or if there are hidden barriers that need to be addressed:

- *Does your company have clear and enforceable policies on discrimination, harassment, and bias?*

- *Are employees of different backgrounds, races, genders, and abilities equally represented in leadership and decision-making positions?*

- *Have you or a colleague ever witnessed or experienced workplace harassment, microaggressions, or exclusionary behavior?*

- *Is there a wage gap in your organization based on gender, race, or other identity factors?*

- *Does your workplace make accommodations for individuals with disabilities or specific needs?*

- *When hiring and promoting employees, does your company ensure that decisions are made based on merit rather than unconscious bias or favoritism?*

- *Does your company offer DEIA training?*

- *Are employees from diverse backgrounds encouraged to share their perspectives and ideas without fear of retaliation or dismissal?*

- *Are complaints related to discrimination and harassment taken seriously?*

- *Does your company participate in broader social responsibility initiatives that promote equity and ethics in the community?*

Ensuring that DEIA initiatives are implemented is essential to foster an ethical workplace. At the same time, businesses also have a broader responsibility that extends beyond their employees and into the world around them. A company's ethical impact is not limited to internal policies; it also includes how it interacts with the environment, the communities it serves, and the industries it influences. In the next chapter, you will explore the responsible impact on the surrounding environment that a business must have. You will get to understand how companies can operate sustainably and maintain ethical standards.

Chapter 7:

Responsible Impact on the

Surrounding Environment

Workplace ethics extend beyond the treatment of employees and the enforcement of fair labor practices. A company's ethical responsibility also includes how it interacts with the environment and its surrounding communities. While sustainability initiatives and corporate social responsibility programs are now common talking points, they are only one part of the community. Childcare, education, and community development are all aspects that ethical employers are concerned with. History has shown that companies have often prioritized profit over environmental and community well-being. In many (if not all) cases, the consequences were devastating.

To illustrate this, consider a town built around a major manufacturing plant. For decades, the factory provided stable jobs, boosting the local economy. However, over time, residents noticed a troubling trend: an increase in respiratory illnesses, unusual cancer cases, and contaminated water supplies. It was later discovered that the plant had been improperly disposing of toxic waste, poisoning the same community that depended on it for employment. This is not just a hypothetical scenario; it echoes real-world environmental disasters where corporate negligence has devastated lives, leaving workers and families to bear the consequences.

Acting unethically is a problem that highlights the short-sighted, profit-first viewpoint that unethical employers can develop. Ensuring the surrounding community's well-being is essential for the employer to have a strong, local workforce from which to recruit. Ethical employers understand that the long-term viability of the organization depends on this and actively work to participate in protecting it.

In today's world, employees are becoming increasingly aware of their employer's impact on the physical environment around them. Companies that disregard sustainability risk losing consumer trust and the loyalty of their workforce. More workers are seeking employers whose values align with their own, recognizing that their well-being is tied not just to wages and benefits, but also to the environmental conditions they live in.

Historical Employer Neglect

You are about to see examples of corporate environmental neglect after environmental concerns were recognized by governmental bodies globally. These disasters may have shaped regulations and the role of government intervention in holding companies accountable. At the same time, even after international environmental concerns are acknowledged, unethical environmental practices in pursuit of profit continue to be frequent.

It is essential to understand what made these actions unethical, and the countless others like them. They represent willful neglect in the face of known or new realities and the arrogance of the employer, through empowered management, ignoring the warnings coming from the workforce. The culmination of both unethical practices and willful ignorance, in several cases, resulted in loss of life and long-term catastrophic damage to the environment and impacted communities.

BP Deepwater Horizon Spill (2010)

The BP Deepwater Horizon explosion in 2010 stands as one of the worst environmental disasters in modern history. The explosion killed 11 workers and spilled over 134 million gallons of crude oil into the Gulf of Mexico, leading to irreparable harm to marine life, coastal economies, and local fishing industries (*Deepwater Horizon Oil Spill*, 2016). Cleanup workers were exposed to toxic chemicals, leading to long-term health issues.

Investigations later revealed that BP had ignored critical safety warnings, opting for cheaper, riskier solutions to speed up oil extraction. Rather than implementing the necessary safety measures, the company prioritized cost savings. In the aftermath, BP engaged in greenwashing, spending millions on marketing campaigns that emphasized its sustainability commitment while continuing unethical environmental practices. The spill exposed the severe consequences of corporate negligence and remains a key example of why environmental regulations are necessary.

In response to public backlash over environmental disasters, many corporations engage in *greenwashing*, a deceptive strategy where companies present themselves as environmentally responsible while continuing harmful practices. These include oil companies that invest in renewable energy projects while expanding fossil fuel extraction, fast fashion brands that promote sustainable clothing lines while maintaining exploitative supply chains, and tech giants that pledge carbon neutrality while operating data centers that consume vast amounts of energy. Greenwashing allows companies to avoid genuine accountability, misleading consumers and employees into believing sustainability is a priority. Recognizing these tactics is essential for holding corporations accountable and demanding real change.

Chernobyl (1986)

The Chernobyl nuclear disaster in 1986 is still one of the most severe industrial accidents in history. A flawed reactor design and improperly trained personnel caused a massive explosion at reactor 4 of the Chernobyl Nuclear Power Plant in Ukraine, releasing deadly radiation into the atmosphere. The Soviet government initially tried to cover up the disaster, delaying evacuations and downplaying the risks.

Thousands of plant workers and first responders suffered from acute radiation sickness, and entire communities had to be abandoned. The long-term effects included increased cancer rates, birth defects, and environmental contamination that persists today. This disaster is a clear example of how corporate and governmental negligence can lead to long-lasting devastation. The failure to enforce strict safety standards led to irreversible consequences, reinforcing the need for proper oversight in industries dealing with hazardous materials.

Bhopal Gas Tragedy (1984)

One of the deadliest industrial disasters in history happened in Bhopal, India, when a Union Carbide pesticide plant leaked 45 tons of methyl isocyanate gas into surrounding neighborhoods (The Editors of Encyclopædia Britannica, 2025a). Within hours, thousands of people died, and hundreds of thousands suffered from long-term health complications, including blindness, respiratory diseases, and neurological disorders.

Investigations revealed that the company had failed to maintain essential safety measures. Cost-cutting led to the removal of key warning systems and safety redundancies, allowing the gas leak to spread unchecked. Survivors and their families continue to fight for justice decades later, as the site remains contaminated and its effects linger in the community.

Mariana Dam Disaster (2015)

On November 5, 2015, a dam owned by Samarco, a joint venture between Vale and BHP Billiton, collapsed in Mariana, Brazil, unleashing 60 million cubic meters of toxic mine waste into the Doce River (Curtis et al., 2024). The flood of sludge destroyed entire villages, killing 19 people instantly and displacing thousands. The toxic waste contaminated local water supplies, affecting hundreds of thousands of residents and causing long-term environmental damage.

This disaster highlighted the dangers of poor regulatory enforcement in the mining industry. Despite warnings about structural weaknesses in the dam, no corrective action was taken. The aftermath saw one of the largest environmental lawsuits in Brazilian history, but affected communities are still struggling to recover nearly a decade later. The Mariana disaster is a tragic example of what happens when corporations neglect environmental and worker safety standards.

Kingston Coal Ash Spill (2008)

In 2008, the Kingston Fossil Plant in Tennessee, operated by the Tennessee Valley Authority, experienced a catastrophic operational failure. Over 1.1 billion gallons of coal ash slurry flooded local rivers and neighborhoods, covering homes and landscapes with toxic sludge (*Coal Ash Spill Cleanup Slow*, 2009). The coal ash, a byproduct of burning coal for electricity, contains heavy metals like arsenic, lead, and mercury, which pose severe health risks. The cleanup efforts exposed workers to dangerous conditions, leading to respiratory diseases and other illnesses. The disaster shed light on weak U.S. environmental regulations for industrial waste disposal, highlighting the need for stronger protections.

These disasters—and many more—demonstrate the consequences of corporate negligence. Without strict regulations and enforcement, companies have repeatedly placed profits above environmental and workers' safety, causing irreparable harm to communities worldwide. In response, governments have established regulatory agencies to monitor environmental impact, enforce corporate responsibility, and prevent future disasters. The next section will explore how agencies such as the U.S. Environmental Protection Agency (EPA), the European Environment Agency (EEA), and Australia's Department of Climate Change are working to hold corporations accountable and promote environmental responsibility.

Shift Toward Greater Corporate Accountability

The impact of environmental disasters has pushed governments worldwide to implement strict regulatory frameworks to hold corporations accountable. Companies have historically cut corners without enforcement, leading to catastrophic events that harm workers, communities, and ecosystems. Recognizing this, multiple regulatory agencies have been established to monitor environmental compliance, enforce penalties, and prevent future disasters.

These agencies have a crucial role in ensuring industries operate responsibly, balancing economic growth with environmental stewardship. Their regulation influences corporate behavior and protects workers and local communities from preventable harm. Read on to learn about key agencies and legislative measures designed to enforce this accountability in environmental protection.

EPA

The U.S. EPA was established in 1970 in response to growing public concern over pollution and industrial waste. The agency enforces laws such as the Clean Air Act and the Clean Water Act, ensuring companies limit their environmental footprint and follow strict operational guidelines. The agency has been essential in holding companies accountable by issuing fines and sanctions for violations. In 2015, Volkswagen was fined $14.7 billion for violating emissions regulations, highlighting that even powerful multinational companies should not be above the law (U.S. Department of Justice, 2016). The EPA's continuous enforcement of pollution limits, waste disposal protocols, and industrial safety regulations ensures businesses meet a minimum acceptable environmental impact standard.

EEA

The EEA plays a significant role in shaping environmental policies across 32 European countries. Established in 1994, it collects data, monitors industrial activities, and ensures businesses comply with E.U. environmental laws. One of the agency's landmark efforts is the European Green Deal, which aims for carbon neutrality by 2050 (European Commission, 2025). This has led to stricter corporate emissions targets, pushing industries toward renewable energy, sustainable manufacturing, and cleaner production processes. Companies that fail to meet these regulations face hefty fines and operational restrictions, reinforcing that sustainability is no longer optional but a legal and ethical need.

Australia's Department of Climate Change

Over time, Australia has been severely affected by corporate environmental negligence, with major disasters such as oil spills, mining pollution, and deforestation affecting communities and biodiversity. In response, the government created the Department of Climate Change, Energy, the Environment, and Water in 2022, which enforces policies ensuring companies operate responsibly. The agency has played an essential role in implementing strict environmental impact assessments that businesses must pass before beginning large-scale projects. In industries like mining and energy, where environmental risks are high, the assessments prevent reckless corporate practices that could lead to catastrophic disasters.

Brazil's IBAMA

Brazil's Instituto Brasileiro do Meio Ambiente e dos Recursos Naturais (Brazilian Institute of the Environment and Natural Resources [IBAMA]) is a key regulatory agency that enforces environmental laws, particularly mining, agriculture, and manufacturing sectors. Given the country's vast Amazon rainforest, the agency has been essential in preventing legal deforestation, pollution, and hazardous industrial waste dumping. The agency gained international attention for its fines and shutdowns of companies involved in illegal Amazon deforestation (Spring, 2021). However, IBAMA faces challenges, including corporate lobbying and political interference, showing that regulatory agencies must continuously fight against economic pressures to protect the environment.

China's Ministry of Ecology and Environment

As one of the world's largest industrial economies, China has experienced severe environmental crises due to unchecked corporate pollution. The Ministry of Ecology and Environment (MEE) was established in 2014 to regulate emissions, monitor industrial waste management, and implement climate policies that mitigate corporate environmental damage (Duggan, 2014). In recent years, the MEE has imposed record-breaking fines on major polluters and introduced strict air quality regulations in response to the country's smog and pollution issues. While enforcement remains a challenge, the MEE's increased efforts are a sign that the world's most industrialized nation is taking steps toward greater corporate accountability.

The establishment of environmental regulatory agencies worldwide reflects the growing recognition that corporate responsibility must extend beyond profits. These agencies play a critical role in ensuring that companies operate ethically. At the same time, enforcement alone is not enough. True change for ethical workplaces requires a cultural shift in corporate values, where environmental ethics become embedded in business operations.

Why This Matters to Workers

For employees, corporate environmental responsibility is not just a legal issue; it is a basic needs issue. Unethical employers damage the employer/employee relationship and undermine a strong work ethic when they endanger families and the surrounding community through willful ignorance and unethical practices. They could also be damaging their employees' ethical beliefs, who are unknowingly participating in unethical actions.

Exposure to pollutants, hazardous waste, and potential industrial accidents may be risks that a properly compensated employee is willing to take, but are they being compensated for their families and communities to take on that risk as well?

Regardless of whether it is through direct exposure to hazardous conditions, job insecurity due to environmental mismanagement, or long-term health effects caused by pollution, the community suffers. Ethical employers understand that being accountable for their environmental impact is not just about the organization's sustainability—it is about the legacy that the organization develops in the community.

Health Risks

For many industries, environmental hazards are intertwined with workplace safety. Employees working in factories, mines, oil refineries, and construction sites face direct exposure to toxic chemicals, polluted air, and hazardous waste. When companies fail to follow proper environmental regulations, these workers are at an increased risk of respiratory diseases, cancer, and other long-term health conditions.

One of the most alarming examples is the Flint water crisis in Michigan (2014–2016). While this disaster primarily affected residents, many city workers and employees in local industries suffered from lead poisoning due to contaminated water. Despite clear warnings about water quality, government officials and corporate contractors ignored the risks, leading to a widespread human-created public health emergency. This crisis demonstrated how environmental neglect directly harms workers and the communities they serve.

Another case is asbestos exposure in industrial and construction sites. For decades, companies ignored the dangers of asbestos fibers, causing lung disease and mesothelioma. Even after regulations were introduced, some businesses continued using asbestos-containing materials, endangering workers. This negligence resulted in thousands of deaths and billions of dollars in lawsuits, proving that protecting the environment is directly tied to protecting human lives.

Job Security

A company's environmental reputation can also determine its economic survival, directly impacting workers. Businesses that engage in environmentally unethical conduct often face fines, shutdowns, and loss of consumer trust, leading to layoffs and financial instability. Workers have a vested interest in ensuring their employees comply with environmental regulations, as companies that operate ethically are more likely to have long-term stability and financial security.

During the Deepwater Horizon oil spill, BP faced massive legal penalties and reputational damage. The disaster affected the environment and led to economic devastation for thousands of oil workers. Most lost their jobs due to BP's financial instability, while others had to endure dangerous cleanup efforts that exposed them to toxic chemicals.

Similarly, in the automotive industry, car manufacturers that fail to comply with emissions standards can face lawsuits and factory closures, putting thousands of jobs at risk. The Volkswagen emissions scandal led to layoffs across multiple countries. Had Volkswagen prioritized ethical environmental practices, its employees would not have had to bear the financial consequences of corporate deception.

Long-Term Impact

Workers do not operate in isolation; they are part of larger communities that suffer when corporations neglect environmental responsibility. When companies pollute rivers, contaminate the air, or engage in irresponsible waste disposal, the impact extends beyond the employees. Instead, it affects families, local businesses, and future generations.

One striking example is the Love Canal disaster in New York, where a chemical company dumped toxic waste into a residential neighborhood. Many workers at the company were unaware of the long-term environmental damage until their own families suffered from severe illnesses, birth defects, and cancers. The tragedy highlighted how corporate negligence can come full circle, harming employees and their loved ones.

In the coal industry, mining towns have experienced severe environmental damage due to reckless corporate practices. The failure to properly dispose of mining waste has led to contaminated drinking water, deadly landslides, and increased health risks for miners and their families. In some cases, like the Mariana disaster, entire communities have been forced to relocate due to environmental degradation, destroying generations of economic and cultural stability.

Your Role in Demanding Accountability

Workers are not powerless when it comes to environmental responsibility. You have the right to demand better protections, report unsafe practices, and advocate for corporate accountability. Many environmental reforms have only happened because workers spoke out against hazardous conditions. Holding employers accountable for environmental responsibility is not just about saving the planet. It is also about ensuring safe workplaces, protecting jobs, and preserving communities for future generations. When companies prioritize environmental ethics, everyone benefits.

For instance, whistleblowers in chemical plants and oil refineries have exposed illegal dumping of toxic waste, leading to stricter environmental regulations. Employee-led movements have also pushed companies to adopt clean energy initiatives, sustainable manufacturing, and better waste management practices. But what about your company? Is your employer truly concerned with the community or simply engaging in greenwashing? Reflect on the questions that follow to decide.

Reflection: Is Your Workplace Environmentally Responsible?

Understanding corporate environmental responsibility goes beyond company slogans and marketing. True employer ethics require action, transparency, and accountability. Use the following questions to evaluate whether your workplace is genuinely committed to protecting the environment or simply engaging in surface-level greenwashing:

- *Does my employer have clear environmental policies in place, and are they actively enforced in daily operations?*

- *Does the company prioritize sustainable practices, such as reducing waste, conserving energy, or using environmentally friendly materials?*

- *Are employees trained on environmental responsibility, including how to minimize their impact at work?*

- *Has the company been involved in environmental violations, and if so, how has it responded to correct its actions?*

- *Are there transparent sustainability reports or public commitments to environmental responsibility?*

- *Does my employer engage in community or government initiatives to improve environmental conditions in the surrounding area?*

- *Are employees encouraged to raise concerns about environmental risks, and is there a system in place to report violations without fear of retaliation?*

- *Does the company hold its suppliers and business partners to the same environmental standards?*

- *Is my workplace considering long-term sustainability solutions, such as adopting renewable energy sources or reducing carbon emissions?*

Employees assume that an employer is concerned with creating a safe and secure workspace, an accountable professional relationship, and having a responsible impact on the surrounding environment. After all, it is not until proven otherwise that any issues need to be addressed. However, it is the transactional nature of employment that the employee–employer relationship is based on and has the biggest impact on work ethic. In the next chapter, we will see how a community-supporting wage is the foundation of employment relationships.

Chapter 8:

Community-Supporting Wage

The discussion around the value of work is usually framed around providing financial stability in getting one's needs met. This is partially true: It is both financial and schedule stability that is required to ensure that anyone can meet their needs. As discussed previously, the primary resource to meet our basic needs is money, and the primary resource to meet our higher needs is time. When wages are too low, it forces workers to sacrifice one need in the pursuit of meeting the other. This is not freedom as envisioned by Maslow; this is the foundation of an abusive relationship.

When workers are paid ethically, they have both the time and the money to meet their needs, which contributes to the local economy and fosters community growth. Ethical workplaces recognize that wages are not just a private financial matter; they have a ripple effect on the well-being of entire neighborhoods, cities, and economies. A community-supporting wage ensures that workers can afford to live where they work, shop at local businesses, invest in their children's education, and participate in civil life.

Consider Maria, a single mother working in food service. She clocks in over 40 hours a week at a fast food chain, yet her paycheck barely covers rent and utilities. To afford childcare and groceries, she takes on a second job cleaning offices late at night, leaving her only a few hours of sleep before doing it all over again. With little time or energy left, Maria is unable to engage in her child's school activities, support local businesses, or contribute to her community in meaningful ways. She does not have the money or time to invest in anything in the community beyond trying to meet her and her family's basic needs. This all too common occurrence is forcing her to sacrifice time with her children, and forcing her children to sacrifice time with her.

When an employer prioritizes ethical community-supporting wages, it reduces employee turnover, fosters loyalty, and creates an environment where workers can actively engage with and give back to their surroundings. This broadens the tax base of support for public needs that local government depends on while reducing stress on social assistance programs. It stabilizes local economies by empowering more consumers to spend at local small businesses. It builds communities as people have the time to participate in local events.

However, ethical wages have not always been the norm. Throughout history, employers have exploited workers through low pay, harsh conditions, and a lack of rights. The fight for ethical wages has been ongoing, requiring government intervention, labor movements, and collective action. This chapter will explore the importance of community-supporting wages and how past practices have shaped modern labor.

A History of Wage Exploitation

Wages have long been a source of struggle for working people. There is a well-documented history of employers prioritizing profit over human dignity. From slavery to company towns, the roots of wage exploitation run deep. However, here we are focusing on the impact of the Industrial Revolution—a period marked by immense technological advancement and also deep human cost.

In the late 18th and 19th centuries, factory workers, including children, were often forced to work 12- to 16-hour shifts in dangerous conditions for a small pay. The new emerging capitalist structure focused on factory-supported mass production, allowing unskilled business owners to generate immense wealth while their skilled employees lived in poverty. This imbalance led to early labor movements, where workers began recognizing that their collective voices were the only defense against the unchecked power of wealth.

The three things empowered the pushback against wealth that we see today. Public education, especially in reading, photography, and increasing communication speed. These three things increased public awareness and fueled outrage against exploitation. One of the earliest examples is the 1911 Triangle Shirtwaist Factory Fire, which exposed the harsh reality of sweatshop labor in the US. The factory's mostly immigrant female workers were locked inside during the fire, resulting in almost 150 deaths, many of which could have been avoided had the employer implemented basic safety measures and respected labor rights (*Triangle Shirtwaist Factory Fire*, 2025). This would have been a local issue before the turn of the century, but both word and picture were quickly spread throughout the country. The demand for change grew in the face of national pressure, forcing the government to respond, eventually leading to the National Labor Relations Act.

Wage exploitation has often gone hand in hand with violent union busting—a tactic used by employers to break up organized labor efforts. The early 1900s saw companies like Ford Motor Company, Republic Steel, and Colorado Fuel and Iron use private security forces, local police, and in some cases the National Guard to intimidate, harass, and even violently attack workers attempting to organize for better pay and working conditions. Since the passage of the National Labor Relations, in 1935, which was meant to protect the right to organize, employers have continued to use legal loopholes, propaganda, and political lobbying to undercut labor power.

Throughout the 20th century and into the present, employers have continued to engage in practices that minimize wage growth. One common method is wage stagnation: refusing to keep wages at a level that is, at a minimum, adjusted to meet the local inflation. Wage stagnation due to technological advancement is also an issue. According to data from Cooper & Kroeger (2017), productivity in the US grew in the past decades, yet hourly pay for typical workers increased less than 20% during the same period. Meanwhile, executive compensation soared, highlighting the growing gap between corporate profits and employee well-being.

Another tactic is the misclassification of workers to avoid providing benefits. For example, as we discussed, many gig companies label their workers as "independent contractors," denying them access to wage protections, health insurance, or job security. "Food and drink service workers make up over a quarter (25.9 percent) of all workers suffering minimum wage violations—the largest share of any single industry," (Cooper & Kroeger, 2017). The irony is that a healthy service industry reflects a healthy community because it highlights a moderate level of disposable income.

Wage theft is another persistent issue. Unethical employers withhold overtime pay, demand that employees work off the clock, and violate wage laws. This costs workers and their local communities between $8 and $15 billion annually (Cooper & Kroeger, 2017). These violations often go unreported due to fear of retaliation or a lack of resources to pursue legal recourse.

Though labor victories have been won and regulations introduced, wage exploitation still lingers. Accepting this history is key to recognizing the importance of policy, advocacy, and ethical leadership in building a future where all workers can earn a wage that supports their needs, which fosters a community's well-being.

Government Intervention

Wage exploitation is not simply a product of unethical practices; it is also the result of the absence of effective regulation and accountability. Over the last century, world governments and labor institutions have stepped in to create safeguards against extreme underpayment, more specifically by establishing minimum wage laws. These serve as the legal floor for what workers can be paid, aiming to protect employees, particularly those in low-wage sectors, from falling into poverty despite full-time work. A small exemplification of these governmental interventions includes the agencies you will see in the following sections.

Fair Labor Standards Act (US)

In the US, the Wage and Hour Division of the Department of Labor enforces the Fair Labor Standards Act (FLSA), which established a federal minimum wage in 1938. Over time, the FLSA has expanded to include protections such as overtime pay and child labor laws. However, the federal minimum wage has remained stagnant at $7.25 since 2009, despite rising inflation and cost-of-living pressures. This has prompted many states and cities to enact, on their own, higher minimum wages. For example, California has set a $16 minimum wage as of 2024, while Washington, D.C. has raised it to over $17.00 per hour.

Living Wage Commission (UK)

The UK's Living Wage Commission was created to address the gap between the legally minimum required wage and the actual cost of living. While the National Minimum Wage ensures basic wage protections, the Real Living Wage is based on what individuals and families truly need to live with dignity. While a voluntary standard promoted by the commission, over 14,000 U.K. employers currently adopt the Real Living Wage, including major corporations, universities, and health care providers.

Fair Work (Australia)

In Australia, Fair Work plays a similar role to a governmental agency. It annually sets and reviews the national minimum wage, considering economic conditions and living standards. As of July 2024, Australia's national minimum wage is $24.10 per hour, one of the highest in the world. This reflects the country's legislative commitment to ensuring that employment is not only a means of survival but also the foundation for a healthy and engaged life.

Mindestlohnkommission (Germany)

The Mindestlohnkommission (Minimum Wage Commission) in Germany was established to guide the implementation of the country's statutory minimum wage, which was first introduced in 2015. The minimum wage is adjusted regularly, reaching €12.82 per hour in 2025. Germany's intervention is also a reflection of a broader European effort to address wage inequality, especially in the aftermath of the global economic crisis.

International Labor Organization

Another key player fighting for ethical wages is the UN's International Labor Organization (ILO), which sets international labor standards and advocates for decent working conditions globally. While it does not impose legal minimum wages, the ILO works closely with governments to ensure that wage policies align with social justice and economic development. It encourages discussions between governments, workers, and employers to reach ethical wage agreements.

These interventions demonstrate that ethical compensation is not a private negotiation, but rather a public responsibility. Governments worldwide have realized that underpayment affects communities, deepening inequality and placing pressure on social safety nets. However, enforcement remains challenging, especially in informal labor sectors, gig work, and industries with low union representation.

While the presence of minimum wage laws is a critical step toward ethical workplaces, their effectiveness is deeply related to the actual cost of living. Many minimum wage earners still struggle to cover rent, food, transportation, and health care, living little to nothing for emergencies or investments in areas such as education. This gap between reality and ethical action requires a closer look to understand how unethical wages affect families and communities as a whole.

Cost of Living vs. the Labor Market

Employers get away with undervaluing their employees by arguing they are being labor market competitive. It is not their fault that they are paying low wages, but the labor market's fault for taking what is offered. This allows them to ignore their responsibility for the financial health of their community. The problem with the argument is that they have the time to wait for the employee who either can or must accept low wages. This pits married couples against single moms, those with student debt against those with none, and high school students against the elderly, all to the advantage of the employer.

The result is a sobering picture of economic instability. In 2022, it was reported that nearly 40% of Americans could not afford a $400 emergency without borrowing or selling something (Daniel, 2023). For workers with families, this insecurity compounds, as covering health insurance, education, groceries, and utilities on low wages becomes a juggling act of sacrifice. Parents often forgo time with children, medical treatment, or even food just to cover bills.

This is particularly evident in the rise of multi-income households. Millions of Americans currently hold more than one job due to the unethical wage practices of employers. Many of these people are working full-time roles supplemented by a combination of part-time employment and gig work, such as food delivery, ride-sharing, or freelance labor, to cover gaps that a single income cannot fill. While the gig economy offers flexibility, it often lacks benefits, job security, and predictable income, making it an unreliable long-term solution for financial stability.

The situation, however, is not limited to the US. The same can be seen in the UK, where real wages have decreased over time, meaning that even when salaries rise, the purchasing power of workers declines due to inflation (Bruce & Milliken, 2024). In cities like London, where average rent is over £2,000 per month, minimum wage workers must often rely on government aid or shared housing to survive. This situation becomes even more critical for immigrants and other groups who work in lower-paying jobs.

For blue-collar workers, the struggle is even more pronounced. Many of these employees face physically demanding labor for wages that barely meet the rising cost of living. In industries where wages are not adjusted for inflation or regional living standards, financial stress becomes a daily burden. These are the same workers who were labeled as "essential" during crises like the COVID-19 pandemic but still continue to earn wages that don't reflect the cost of that essentiality.

This misalignment between ethical compensation and cost creates a precarious cycle: Workers cannot save, invest, or build long-term financial security. It prevents families from buying homes, accessing quality education, or planning for retirement. Instead, they live in constant financial anxiety, vulnerable to any unexpected expense. The reality is that when wages do not rise with the cost of living, it no longer becomes just an economic issue; it also becomes a social and ethical one. If it is expected in a society that the primary way someone can meet their needs is through employment, then that society needs to ensure that employers properly value work.

The Fight for Ethical Wages

The struggle for ethical compensation has been a long-standing issue in the history of labor. While minimum wage laws and government interventions have helped to some extent, they have not fully addressed the underlying disparities in pay, especially for blue-collar and service industry workers. Today, the fight continues in different forms, as employees, advocates, and unions push for ethical wages that provide dignity, stability, and the ability to thrive and support the community.

Gig workers, such as rideshare drivers, delivery couriers, and freelance laborers, have become the new face of wage vulnerability. Because these workers are often classified as independent contractors, they are excluded from traditional labor protections like minimum wage laws, health benefits, and job security. This lack of classification often benefits companies while leaving workers with few legal avenues to demand ethical pay or challenge exploitative practices. The rise of platforms such as Uber, DoorDash, and Instacart has led to growing calls for clearer labor classification and baseline protections for an increasingly essential workforce.

In the hospitality industry, roles like servers, cooks, and dishwashers continually face outdated wage structures. This system assumes that tips will supplement wages, but also relies on the fact that all patrons can afford to tip the server to begin with. Efforts to abolish the tipping wage system are part of a broader movement to standardize compensation across sectors, ensuring a predictable and ethical income floor for all workers.

For those who work in construction, manufacturing, and logistics, the conversation around wages often intersects with overvaluing formal education and undervaluing experience and the physical demands of the work. These industries historically experienced aggressive union busting and wage exploitation tactics, yet have seen a resurgence in labor organization and collective bargaining efforts. From warehouse workers at Amazon to auto workers in Detroit, employees are calling out the gap between increasing company profits and stagnant wages on the shop floor.

As with all employer ethics, a community-supporting wage requires the engagement of the community from the employer, but that is far from enough. It requires society to value the time of every worker, regardless of who they are or what they do. If an orphaned, high school dropout with a criminal record decides they want to change their life and work part-time jobs as a busboy for a couple of diners to get to the equivalent of full-time employment, they should have the time and money for a modest life. They should be able to put food on the table, have a roof over their head, set aside some money for savings, and engage with their local community in whatever positive way they see fit.

When society allows employers to undervalue labor, they not only diminish the worth of the individual; they also undermine the integrity of the workplace and the health of the broader economy. Ethical employers must recognize that compensation is not merely a line item on a budget; it is also a statement about the type of company they choose to be and the type of community they choose to work in. Ethical employers understand that the first relationship that every other relationship is built on is the transactional relationship of employment.

Reflection: Are Your Wages Truly Supporting Your Life?

Ethical compensation is more than a paycheck: It is a foundational element of ethical employment and personal well-being. As companies aim to maintain profitability, employees need to pause and evaluate whether their wages reflect the true value of their labor and allow them to live with stability and dignity. Use the following questions to reflect on your current wage situation. These are designed to apply across industries and job roles, especially for workers in services, trades, gig work, and industry professions:

- *Can I meet monthly living expenses (rent, utilities, food, and transportation) without relying on credit cards or loans?*

- *Am I forced to take on a second job or gig work just to cover the basics?*

- *Does my income allow me to save for emergencies or future goals like education, housing, or retirement?*

- *Have my wages kept pace with inflation or the rising cost of living in my area?*

- *Do I feel ethically compensated compared to others in similar roles or industries?*

- *Am I paid for all the hours I work, including overtime, prep time, or commute-related tasks?*

- *Do I receive additional compensation like tips, commissions, or bonuses? If so, are they consistent and ethical?*

- *Is my wage structure transparent, and do I understand how my pay is determined?*

- *Have I ever felt afraid to ask for a raise or talk about wage concerns with my employer?*

- *Do I believe my employer sees my labor as essential and values it accordingly?*

If your answers raise concerns, you are not alone. Many workers across the world are using the same questions and pushing for wages that reflect the real cost of living and the dignity of their labor. These reflections are not just about money; they are about sustainability, respect, and working in an ethical workplace. The question now is: *How are all these elements directly related to the Maslowian principles?* As you move forward to the next chapter, you will be able to reflect on how ethical employment fits into the equation and how work ethic is more about meeting one's higher needs.

Chapter 9:

The Maslowian Principles

of Employment Ethics

Throughout this book, you have explored the complex and transactional nature of the employer–employee relationship. From understanding that employment is not a favor, but an exchange of time and skill for compensation, to the deeper exploration of work ethic, and the establishment of employer ethics, you have seen the real-world consequences of ethical (and unethical) workplace practices.

You have seen how employees are expected to bring value to their work through productivity, reliability, autonomy, and collaboration. You have also seen how employers need to supply an ethical workspace that provides a safe and secure workspace, a community-supporting wage, a professional accountable relationship, and a responsible impact on their surrounding environment. You now understand how these two aspects of employment ethics are interconnected and build a strong employment relationship.

This chapter brings all these elements together. You will focus on how ethical employment fulfills the levels of Maslow's hierarchy and how an imbalance in the employment relationship prevents workers from advancing, especially when employer ethics fail. Most importantly, you will explore what ethical leadership looks like when it's done right and how you, as a worker, can recognize your value and advocate for a workplace that supports your needs and growth.

Bringing It All Together

Ethical employment is more than just checking off compliance boxes or offering occasional perks. It is also about ensuring that the very structure of a workplace supports the fundamental human needs of its employees. Maslow's Hierarchy of Needs, which was first introduced in Chapter 3, gives us the framework to understand how those needs progress from survival to fulfillment. Now, at the end of this journey, you can bring together everything you have learned about work and workplace ethics by viewing employment through its hierarchy.

As a reminder, the five needs are, in order: physiological, safety and security, love and belonging, esteem, and self-actualization. Physiological and safety and security make up what is referred to as basic needs because they focus on addressing requirements for life and long-term stable access to meet those needs. The needs of love and belonging, esteem, and self-actualization are referred to as higher needs because fulfilling these needs requires interacting with others.

You can identify where in Maslow's pyramid either employment or worker ethics relates best. This is vital in understanding how the needs of both parties interact so that each can work toward meeting the needs of the other and develop a better employment relationship.

Level 1: Psychological Needs—The Foundation of Survival

It is here that the foundation of the employment relationship is laid. Physiological needs represent the ability to sustain oneself through the use of resources. For the employer, this means either converting a resource into a product or providing a service to a client, allowing the organization to continue. The employee's productivity in the role for which they were hired ensures that the physiological needs of the organization are met.

For the employee, this means that they are receiving a community-supporting wage through full-time employment so that they can afford a roof over their head, food on the table, and transportation to and from work, with enough money and time left over to meet the rest of their needs as they see fit in a free and fair society.

However, physiological also means that the surrounding environment is not actively working against them. Employers are ethically required to provide a safe and secure workspace and are responsible for their impact on the surrounding environment. Not addressing safety concerns and polluting the air, water, and soil undermines employees' ability to live safely. This threatens the employer because recruiting and retaining employees will become increasingly difficult.

Level 2: Safety and Security Needs— Stability

Once the physiological needs are met, their long-term stability becomes the focus. This helps alleviate anxieties about those vital needs being threatened again. Employees provide this to their employer through their reliability. This is through not only being reliable in doing the tasks they were hired to do on time and at an acceptable level, but also through showing up when they are scheduled to and informing their employer when they cannot come in for whatever reason.

On the other hand, employers provide a safe and secure workspace by ensuring that a professional relationship is the minimum acceptable standard. Employees will find it difficult to perform to acceptable standards when they feel constantly threatened. It doesn't matter whether the threat is real or not, from their environment or from the people in that environment, and regardless of the threat being to their personal or professional well-being, the threat will always be at the forefront of the employee's mind.

In some cases, this may be a constant part of the job, such as for those who are police officers or firefighters, and the employer should ensure proper training and equipment are supplied to mitigate risk. Even then, if a police officer also learned that their sergeant is a member of a hate group that targets them, or a firefighter who is worried about potential layoffs, this creates an insecure and potentially unsafe work environment for them and everyone around them. This then undermines the employment relationship.

Level 3: Love and Belonging—Trust

At this point, we see the divergence of needs between the employee and the employer. The employee's ethical demands on the employer are focused on addressing their own basic needs, ensuring they can reasonably focus on the task at hand undistracted. However, when it comes to higher needs, employees have the freedom to get those needs met through their work or their life outside of it. This is the level of freedom that Maslow strove for people to understand when he developed his hierarchy of needs.

On the other hand, employers do have some demands for basic needs, but they also require some higher needs. Both autonomy and collaboration fall under the need for love and belonging. Why is that? Because it is at this level that one of the key components of professional relationships is developed in the world of work—trust. Although the transactional relationship of employment also depends on some level of trust between both parties, only the employer depends on the employee developing a relationship outside the employee–employer relationship.

They need each employee to have a level of trust with both their peers and management. This does not mean that the employee needs to be likable; they need to develop a trusted reputation. An ethical workplace environment is one where the workforce and management trust each other, and great strides are made to maintain that trust. This is because, like any structure, it is harder to rebuild trust than maintain it.

This is also where both ought and want to stay with an organization are developed. This is because building a trusting relationship takes time, and leaving that trust can feel like abandonment, even if it is for the better. Relationships are built on true trust and hope for the success of both parties when they part. However, those built on false trust try to reinforce that feeling of abandonment in the other party, inflicting a greater sense of loss.

Level 4: Esteem—Recognition, Achievement, and Growth

When it comes to the final two levels of needs, it is important to understand that how these needs are met is controlled primarily by the employee, not the employer. Some employees may have this need satisfied simply by peer acknowledgment, while some may seek a formal public acknowledgment from their employer. Some may seek esteem from an organization other than their employer, though some may seek it from a loved one. Some may have little value for esteem and instead pursue self-actualization, but even for them, acknowledgment is appreciated.

That being said, the need for esteem in the employee–employer relationship is unique: For employees, it is a need, and for employers, it is a tool. Employers understand that one of the easiest ways to build commitment within employees is by acknowledging their employees' accomplishments. Addressing the need for esteem among employees justifies the investment and development of trust from both the employer and peers. Esteem is one of the easiest tools for an employer to use to develop commitment within their employees. However, that tool can rust when not used enough, and can be seen as a hammer when it is overused.

Level 5: Self-Actualization—Purpose, Fulfillment, and Meaning

At the top of Maslow's hierarchy is self-actualization, or the desire to achieve one's full potential. Although rarely attained through one's employment alone, if an employee is achieving this through their work, there is little an employer can do other than ensure that the employee's basic needs continue to be met. Regardless, employees who can meet the need of self-actualization, whether through their work or outside of it, tend to reflect the highest level of commitment to an employer because the employer is empowering them to meet this need.

These tend to be the people who are considered to have the highest work ethic because they are meeting their highest needs and want to continue to do so. Ethical employers understand that employees who attain this through their work are rare exceptions in the workforce and should be celebrated. Unethical employers overestimate how many people achieve self-actualization through their work and use those who do as the benchmark by which other employees are judged.

When Employer Ethics Fail

While the ideal workplace supports the full spectrum of employee needs—from basic survival to self-actualization—the reality for many workers is far from this vision. Across industries and job types, countless organizations fail to meet even the most fundamental ethical responsibilities. When employer ethics collapse, it isn't just a policy failure, but a personal crisis for the people who rely on those jobs to live.

When a company neglects its ethical obligations, it forces workers into survival mode, often stripping away any chance of growth or security. It may not always look dramatic, and there might not be a catastrophic accident or headline-worthy scandal, but the slow erosion of trust, compensation, and safety creates long-term harm. Corporate greed, cost-cutting disguised as "efficiency," and a culture of silence allow unethical practices to thrive beneath the surface.

Unethical workplaces often mask exploitation with performance language that pits the employees' commitment against their needs. You may hear phrases like "We're family here" or "We expect passion" to justify unpaid overtime, adding on responsibilities, or stagnating compensation. In these environments, loyalty is often demanded but rarely returned. Raises are postponed indefinitely. Safety complaints are ignored. Promotions are promised but never delivered. Recognition is selective or superficial, and workers are left to shoulder the emotional and physical burden.

These failures are not always the result of malicious intent. Sometimes, they stem from incompetence, a lack of accountability, poor leadership, or outdated systems. But the impact is the same. When employees are overworked, underpaid, or unsafe, they cannot even meet the first levels of Maslow's hierarchy, much less pursue anything higher.

The Need for Vigilance

Where there is a lack of employer ethics, vigilance becomes essential. Recognizing the signs of collapsing employer ethics is the first step toward protecting your well-being, and potentially the well-being of others. Some red flags include

- high turnover and burnout among staff

- frequent unpaid labor or underpaid labor

- unsafe working conditions with little follow-up

- discrimination or harassment that goes unaddressed

- vague communication around wages, scheduling, or policies

- a culture of favoritism or inconsistency in leadership

- expansion of duties and responsibilities without proper compensation

If these situations sound familiar, it may be time to ask hard questions: Is this job serving your long-term needs? Are you constantly operating in crisis mode just to stay employed? Are your physical, mental, or financial health deteriorating because of your workplace?

The goal of this reflection is not to assign blame but to spark awareness. Many people stay in harmful environments because they feel they have no choice. In some cases, options may be limited due to economic conditions, caregiving responsibilities, or local job markets. But even with these constraints, knowledge is power. Understanding what ethical employment should look like gives you the tools to make informed decisions—whether that means speaking up, seeking support, advocating for change, or planning your exit strategy.

At the organizational level, unethical practices do not just hurt employees; they also weaken the company. High turnover, disengagement, reputational damage, and reduced productivity are all symptoms of neglected ethics. Eventually, these companies pay the price, whether through lawsuits, loss of public trust, or mass resignation. For workers, knowing your value is the starting point for protecting it. You are not just a number on a schedule or a body in a uniform. Your time, energy, and skill deserve ethical treatment.

Employment should not come at the cost of your dignity, health, or future.

A Vision for the Future

Imagine a small manufacturing company in the Midwestern US called Horizon Tools. For years, it operated like many others in the industry: long hours, high turnover, modest pay, and management disconnected from the realities of the shop floor. Productivity was decent, but morale was low. People came and went. Then, a shift began with leadership— one that recognized that business success is directly tied to ethical employment practices.

The new CEO did not arrive with grand slogans or flashy corporate speak. Instead, she started by listening. She held town halls with floor workers, drivers, machine operators, and custodial staff. She asked questions such as, "What do you need to do your job better?" "What is keeping you up at night?" "What would make you proud to work here?" From those conversations, Horizon began a quiet but powerful transformation.

Wages were adjusted not to be market competitive, but to allow for at least a middle-class living based on the cost of living in the area for all employees. New safety protocols were introduced not because of OSHA requirements, but because leadership recognized that every injury was a human cost, not just a liability.

The HR department was restructured to focus on employee advocacy. A culture of transparency replaced top-down directives. Supervisors were trained in compliance, communication, and emotional intelligence. Opportunities for advancement were opened to every employee, regardless of title or background. One employee, Khalid, who started as a janitor, was offered mentorship after suggesting a more efficient workflow for packing and distribution. Two years later, he became a supervisor respected for his work ethic, insight, humility, and collaborative spirit.

At Horizon, productivity and satisfaction rose. Absenteeism dropped. Retention climbed. Customers noticed a difference in service and quality. And most importantly, the employees began to feel that they mattered, that their work had a purpose, and that their voices were heard.

This isn't a fantasy. Variations of Horizon Tools exist in real life. Companies like Patagonia, Costco, and Interface have built reputations not just for performance but also for treating employees ethically, supporting environmental sustainability, and fostering inclusive cultures. Their success proves that ethical employment is not just good for people; it is also good for business.

In a truly ethical workplace, the relationship between employer and employee is one of mutual accountability. The employer ensures fair wages, safe conditions, respect, and a culture of growth. The employee brings reliability, effort, adaptability, and creativity. Trust replaces fear. Stability replaces burnout. Loyalty becomes something earned, not demanded.

This vision isn't about perfection, it's about intention. It's about building workplaces where ethical treatment is not a perk but the standard. These are places where workers don't have to sacrifice their health or humanity to earn a paycheck. The road ahead won't be easy. It will take advocacy, courage, and cooperation from both sides. But if workers and employees alike commit to building better, more ethical environments, then stories like Horizon's will no longer be the exception; they will be the norm.

So, what should be done, and how should I enforce that my employer has ethical employment practices? In the next and final chapter, you will explore the roles of each party in ensuring employee needs are met and the actions that can be taken to ensure this happens. From acting internally in small groups to evolving governments and agencies, there are different ways to ensure ethical employment practices.

Chapter 10:

The Call to Action

Now it is time to move from awareness to action. Employment ethics is not just a theoretical concept; it is a practical, achievable standard that benefits everyone. When businesses commit to being ethical, safe, and professional, they create better workplaces by building stronger teams, developing a more loyal customer through value alignment, and contributing to healthier, more stable communities. Ethical employers see fewer accidents, lower turnover, greater innovation, and more motivated employees. Workers who feel safe and valued are more motivated, engaged, and fulfilled. Society wins when both sides thrive.

But real, lasting change does not happen by accident; it requires active participation by both the employer and the employee. In this last chapter, you will find the tools to help you understand this role and how to take meaningful steps and hold others accountable. You will find an action plan that outlines what ethical labor looks like and how to make it a reality by starting where you are. Change starts with one person raising their voice, one question being asked, and one step being taken. *You* are that person, so let's get to work.

Employment Ethics and the Role of Government

Workplace regulations exist for a reason. They are the product of decades (often centuries) of advocacy, tragedies, and public outcry. Child labor laws, minimum wage standards, workplace safety guidelines, antidiscrimination protections, and labor rights were not freely given. They were won through struggle, negotiation, and most importantly, legislation. Once they were established, they had to be enforced since, without enforcement, laws are nothing more than words on paper.

As an employee, it is crucial to understand that before government regulation, employees had no way to demand basic human rights. Employers sought out the cheapest willing worker, and every worker was expendable. Now, there is an understanding that the government has a role to play in the establishment and maintenance of baseline employment ethics. While employers may choose to go beyond those standards, it is the government that ensures a common floor, especially in places where workers have little power on their own. It is not optional for employers to provide safe working conditions or pay a minimum wage—it is the law. And when they fail, it is the government's job to step in.

Even in union-friendly environments, the government plays a critical role. Unions are vital, but their reach is limited by membership, region, and political climate.

Not every workplace is unionized, especially gig work, service, and some blue-collar jobs. In fact, few of them are, as they face stiff resistance to organizing. In these cases, it is often only through government oversight that workers can access protections and accountability.

In regions or sectors where unionization is weak or actively discouraged, government regulation becomes even more important. Agencies like the U.S. Department of Labor's Wage and Hour Division, the EEOC, and OSHA exist to ensure that basic employment ethics are not left to the whims of the market. Similar protection exists worldwide, from Canada's Employment and Social Development Department to the UK's HSE. Imagine for a moment what the world would look like without these protections.

Without these governmental agencies, warehouse workers could be scheduled 16 hours straight, without breaks or overtime pay. A restaurant server could be fired for reporting harassment. A construction worker could be forced to operate dangerous machinery without proper safety gear. A pregnant retail worker could be denied bathroom breaks. A factory employing undocumented labor could exploit that status to avoid paying fair wages or maintaining safe conditions—all without consequence.

The reality is that these things still happen, but far less where government oversight is active, well-funded, and taken seriously. Yet, many of the agencies tasked with protecting workers are underfunded, overburdened, or politically limited in what they do. That is why public engagement matters. When workers speak up, when violations are reported, and when lawmakers are pressured to protect basic ethical practices, governments respond, while silence lets unethical practices fester.

As a worker, you do not need to memorize every law or become a legal expert. What you need to do is understand. Understand that you have a right to demand a basic level of ethics from your employer. Recognize that the role of labor departments and watchdog agencies is to enforce and protect those rights. Understand that blood has been spilled and lives were lost in the fight for those protections, and those rights continue to be under threat. Understand that you are not alone in the fight for employer ethics, and that it is the duty of the government and its institutions to be your ally. Understand that when employers fall short of ethical standards when unions are absent or weakened, it is your right to demand that the government fulfills its duty: to hold employers accountable to defend every worker's rights. If the government fails to act, you must advocate for reform.

The Fight for Ethical Wages

Ethical wages are not a luxury. They are a right. While laws and institutions play an important role in ensuring ethical compensation, real change often begins with workers raising their voices. As an employee, you are not powerless. You have the unique perspective and lived experience necessary to drive progress forward.

However, this requires one essential step: setting a universal benchmark.

There is a reason that a community-supporting wage is the standard of an ethical wage. It can be easily calculated. Food on the table, a roof over their head, and transportation to and from work. These variables make up many components of what is considered a living wage, but ignore all but the most basic needs of the employee. A community-supporting wage is a budgetable wage that gives people both the time and money to meet their needs and allows them to be active community members. This is done because a community-supporting wage is based on the average employee following the modern budgetary guidelines of the 50-30-20 rule.

This rule states that of your take-home pay, 50% of your income should go to your needs (the cost of an average healthy month of meals, a single bedroom apartment, and transportation to and from work), 30% of your budget goes to your wants, and 20% of your budget goes to savings and security. Then, by adding local, state, and federal taxes back, it can set the average cost to live in the community surrounding the employer.

This budgetary practice falls in line with Maslowian thinking because it allows one of the most important freedoms that a living wage does not, the freedom of sacrifice. A living wage does not allow for the freedom to move any funds around to save more or pursue or get a better education in a meaningful way. The unfortunate side effect for those at or below a living wage is that those who are receiving it are already sacrificing for their employer, and it is not being acknowledged. This makes it extremely difficult to make any gains without more personal and extreme sacrifices.

This is why fighting for ethical wages matters so deeply. Here are a few ways to help you achieve this objective:

- **Open wage talks:** Share with your peers what you are making and ask the same of them. Employers depend on employees avoiding the wage discussion to avoid equitable compensation.

- **Hold the line:** When asked to take on more responsibilities, ensure that you are properly compensated if they go beyond the job you were hired to do. Remember, free work is never fair work.

- **Whistleblowing:** If your employer is violating wage laws, misclassifying workers, or avoiding overtime pay, you can anonymously report these issues to labor boards or watchdog organizations. It is not a betrayal, but a protection, not just for you, but also for others like you.

The fight for ethical wages is part of a larger fight for dignity, stability, and opportunity. It begins with recognizing your worth, raising concerns when things are wrong, and standing with others who do the same. When workers speak out together, employers, industries, and even governments start to listen.

How to Advocate for Change

Knowing something isn't right at work is the first step, but knowing what to do is just as important. Regardless of whether these are unethical wages, unsafe conditions, or discrimination, this is how change begins. While it can feel overwhelming, there are clear tools and protections available to you.

Recognizing ethical failures is important, but knowing what to do about them is even more crucial. Here are a few steps you can take to advocate for yourself:

- **Document everything**: If you suspect unethical workplace practices, keep a record of incidents, conversations, and patterns. This will be valuable if you need to escalate your concerns. This includes

    - **Forwarding to yourself relevant communication**: Do not depend on the company-provided email system or company phones for any communications. If they set it up, they have access to it and control of it.

    - **Witnesses**: Ask a friend to join you in the meeting. Ask that they be a silent witness and possibly take notes in the meeting.

    - **Record meetings**: Verify local law in your area about whose approval is needed to record a meeting, but even then, be willing to record a meeting and get people on record demanding that the recording be turned off.

- ○ **Contemporaneous notes:** If none of the previous things are available to you, contemporaneous notes are. As soon as you can, after a meeting, write down everything you can remember. Include the date and approximate time of the meeting, who was there, and what was talked about. Try to give as much detail as possible, including key points, and any comments that stick out or can be quoted.

- **Speak up:** Managerial incompetence is actually a start of good-faith discussions. Maybe they honestly don't know something, and no one has brought it up before. Honest and open communication is vital for any organization. Problems arise when incompetence turns into willful ignorance. This is when you may need to escalate the issue to the next level, be that a supervisor, the HR department, or an external agency. Many workers worry that speaking out will jeopardize their jobs. While that fear is valid, retaliation is a serious offense, and legal protection exists for whistleblowers. Knowing this helps shift the power balance back in your favor.

- **Seek collective support:** Do not assume you are alone in your concerns; discuss them with colleagues. Try to bring concern forward as a group because a collective voice is often stronger than an individual one voice is often stronger than an individual one. If your concerns are being ignored, you might also want to consider seeking support in a union, as they are still one of the strongest tools for collective bargaining and protection. Even if you are not unionized, you can support union efforts, learn from organizers, and explore ways to initiate organizing in your industry or region.

- **Know your rights:** Research labor laws and workplace protections relevant to your industry. If necessary, consult a labor rights organization or seek legal advice. Government websites, nonprofit worker advocacy groups, and community legal clinics are excellent sources of information. Take time to learn your rights, which in turn, will help you know the rights of your fellow employees. That knowledge may help you discover that you are not alone and that others are dealing with the same challenges.

- **Consider your options:** Are you targeting the right people to influence change? Can you find a sympathetic ear with an elected representative? What about going public with the issue? Is it even worth the fight if there are other, or better, employment options available?

Holding employers accountable is a major task, but not one you need to do alone. If you are being affected by unethical practices, more than likely, others have too. Also, know that public accountability comes with collective visibility. When workers talk to each other and share experiences, patterns emerge and, with them, the power to act together. Employment ethics is not about punishment, but about building an employment relationship of mutual values and respect.

Change is rarely instant, but it's possible. Start small. Talk to your family and friends first. Ensure that you have a support structure there for you to lean on. Then, start a conversation with coworkers. Share your story and listen to others. Start a coffee group or a controlled chat group so that people can come together and find each other outside of work. Reach out to advocacy groups or legal clinics for advice. Use social media carefully to share your story and reach out to others with similar experiences within other organizations. Although you might feel this way now, you are not alone—you can do this!

Conclusion

Before we go any further, let me thank you for reading this book. This piece of literature was my attempt to reframe the conversation around the world of work. History has proven that one voice can become many, and collective awareness becomes collective action. Unethical employers depend on disjointed voices to maintain a status quo that benefits them. When we have a unified language, it creates a unified message, and a unified message becomes harder for them to resist.

To that end, let's recap what we covered. We worked through what ethical employment really means and what it should look like for every worker, regardless of their work, history, or education. We know the foundational truth: Employment is not a favor or a gift—it's a transactional relationship. This relationship, like every other, comes with a set of expectations for both parties, and both should work to meet them.

You have explored the difference between leadership and management, learning that not every employer or manager is a leader. You also learned that trust must be earned through accountability, not assumed through authority. You also saw the essential human needs as laid out in Maslow's hierarchy, and how every workplace should support those needs through active application of employer ethics.

Throughout the chapters, we focused on employment ethics, the employer–employee relationship, work ethic, and organizational commitment, and established the four components of employer ethic. You learned about the consequences of when these elements are missing and how burnout, discrimination, and underpayment can keep workers in survival mode. However, you have also caught a glimpse of what is possible when things are done right: when companies build cultures of respect, fairness, and empowerment.

Empowerment Is a Process

This cannot be said enough that empowerment is a process. Knowledge and success build momentum and confidence, and missteps and failures build determination and grit. Empowerment does not mean having all the answers today. It means taking action now and working to find the answers tomorrow. This book has helped empower you, and you are now a participant in a much larger conversation. One that, as was highlighted here, has been unfolding for generations and will continue with your voice, your questions, and your decisions.

At this point, you may be assessing your current employment situation and wondering if it is even worth it, if you should stay or go. Let me tell you this, both are the right answers. Both are actions against unethical employment practices. Choosing to walk away from a job, even a toxic one, can be difficult. Knowing your true north and refusing to give ground when it comes to what you stand for is admirable. If this book helped you with that decision either way, I am proud of you and proud to be a part of your decision.

A Collective Mission

Share this book with others. If it helped you see your workplace differently, let it help someone else, too. Talk about it in your employee group chat. Print the reflection questions and post them in your lunchroom. Bring it to your union meeting. Start the conversation, because one voice can become many, and collective awareness becomes collective action.

Every worker deserves an ethical workplace. Every employer has a responsibility to uphold that. And every reader of this book now carries the knowledge to help bridge that gap. You now have a guide. A framework. A tool to reflect, respond, and rise. Let this be the spark, not the end.

Resources

- **Department of Climate Change, Energy, the Environment and Water (Australia):** www.dcceew.gov.au/

- **European Environment Agency:** www.eea.europa.eu/en

- **Fair Work (Australia):** www.fairwork.gov.au/

- **German Social Accident Insurance (DGUV):** www.dguv.de/en/index.jsp

- **Health and Safety Executive (UK):** www.hse.gov.uk/

- **International Organization for Standardization (ISO):** www.iso.org/home.html

- **Mindestlohnkommission (Minimum Wage Commission) (Germany):** www.mindestlohn-kommission.de/EN/Commission

- **Ministry of Ecology and Environment of the People's Republic of China:** english.mee.gov.cn/

- **Occupational Safety and Health Administration:** www.osha.gov/

- **Safe Work Australia:** www.safeworkaustralia.gov.au/

- **U.S. Environmental Protection Agency:** www.epa.gov/

References

Bruce, A., & Milliken, D. (2024, November 12). *UK regular pay grows at slowest pace in two years, pointing to lower inflation.* Reuters. https://www.reuters.com/world/uk/uk-regular-pay-rises-by-annual-48-three-months-september-2024-11-12/

Coal ash spill cleanup slow; cause still unknown. (2009, June 21). NBC News. https://www.nbcnews.com/id/wbna31473983

Cooper, D., & Kroeger, T. (2017, May 10). *Employers steal billions from workers' paychecks each year.* Economic Policy Institute. https://www.epi.org/publication/employers-steal-billions-from-workers-paychecks-each-year/

Curtis, J., Walker, N., & Robinson, T. (2024, October 6). *Mariana Dam disaster.* House of Commons Library. https://commonslibrary.parliament.uk/research-briefings/cdp-2023-0133/

Daniel, W. (2023, May 23). *"Turbulence ahead": Nearly 4 in 10 Americans lack enough money to cover a $400* *emergency expense, Fed survey shows.* Fortune. https://fortune.com/2023/05/23/inflation-economy-consumer-finances-americans-cant-cover-emergency-expense-federal-reserve/

Deepwater Horizon Oil Spill. (2016). National Oceanic and Atmospheric Administration. https://response.restoration.noaa.gov/deepwater-horizon-oil-spill-case-study

Duggan, J. (2014, April 25). China's polluters to face large fines under law change. *The Guardian.* https://www.theguardian.com/environment/chinas-choice/2014/apr/25/china-environment-law-fines-for-pollution

The Editors of Encyclopædia Britannica. (2025a, April 21). Bhopal disaster. In *Encyclopedia Britannica.* https://www.britannica.com/event/Bhopal-disaster

The Editors of Encyclopædia Britannica. (2025b, April 25). Triangle Shirtwaist Factory fire. In *Encyclopedia Britannica.* https://www.britannica.com/event/Triangle-shirtwaist-factory-fire

The European Green Deal. (2025). European Commission. https://commission.europa.eu/strategy-and-policy/priorities-2019-2024/european-green-deal_en

Greenhalgh, N. (2023, June 13). *Leadership vs. management: The key differences.* Daniels College of Business, University of Denver. https://daniels.du.edu/blog/leadership-vs-management/

Greenhouse, S. (2022, November 23). "The success is inspirational": the Fight for $15 movement 10 years on. *The Guardian.* https://www.theguardian.com/us-news/2022/nov/23/fight-for-15-movement-10-years-old

Living Wage Commission. (2025). Living Wage Foundation. https://www.livingwage.org.uk/living-wage-commission

Meindl, J. R., Ehrlich, S. B., & Dukerich, J. M. (1985). The romance of leadership. *Administrative Science Quarterly, 30*(1), 78–102. https://doi.org/10.2307/2392813

Muir, M. (2024, February 19). *Looking to hire based on cultural alignment? Here's what to look for.* Inspiring Workplaces. https://www.inspiring-workplaces.com/content/looking-to-hire-based-on-cultural-alignment-heres-what-to-look-for

Saval, N. (2015, September 8). Don't expect companies to be benevolent. *The New York Times.*

https://www.nytimes.com/roomfordebate/201
5/09/08/can-companies-excel-without-making-
workers-miserable/dont-expect-companies-to-
be-benevolent

Special report: Brand trust in 2020. (2020). Edelman Trust.
https://www.edelman.com/sites/g/files/aatuss
191/files/2020-
06/2020%20Edelman%20Trust%20Barometer
%20Specl%20Rept%20Brand%20Trust%20in%
202020.pdf

Spring, J. (2021, December 21). *Brazil shuts illegal timber
schemes, sheds light on Amazon logging.* Reuters.
https://www.reuters.com/markets/commoditie
s/exclusive-brazil-shuts-illegal-timber-schemes-
sheds-light-amazon-logging-2021-12-21/

U.S. Department of Justice. (2016, June 28). *Volkswagen
to spend up to $14.7 billion to settle allegations of
cheating emissions tests and deceiving customers on 2.0
liter diesel vehicles.* The Department of Justice.
https://www.justice.gov/archives/opa/pr/volk
swagen-spend-147-billion-settle-allegations-
cheating-emissions-tests-and-deceiving

Wages and the Fair Labor Standards Act. (2024). U.S.
Department   of   Labor.
https://www.dol.gov/agencies/whd/flsa

Wetherell, E., & Pendell, R. (2022, March 19). *Only 4 in
10 employees report unethical behavior -- Here's how to*

fix it. Gallup.
https://www.gallup.com/workplace/390635/e
mployees-report-unethical-behavior-fix.aspx

Xiang, N. (2024, December 12). *SHRM report: Workplace culture fosters employee retention worldwide.* SHRM.
https://www.shrm.org/executive-
network/insights/shrm-report-workplace-
culture-fosters-employee-retention

Zaleznik, A. (2004, January). *Managers and leaders: Are they different?* Harvard Business Review.
https://hbr.org/2004/01/managers-and-
leaders-are-they-different